AF575925

Schiffer Publishing

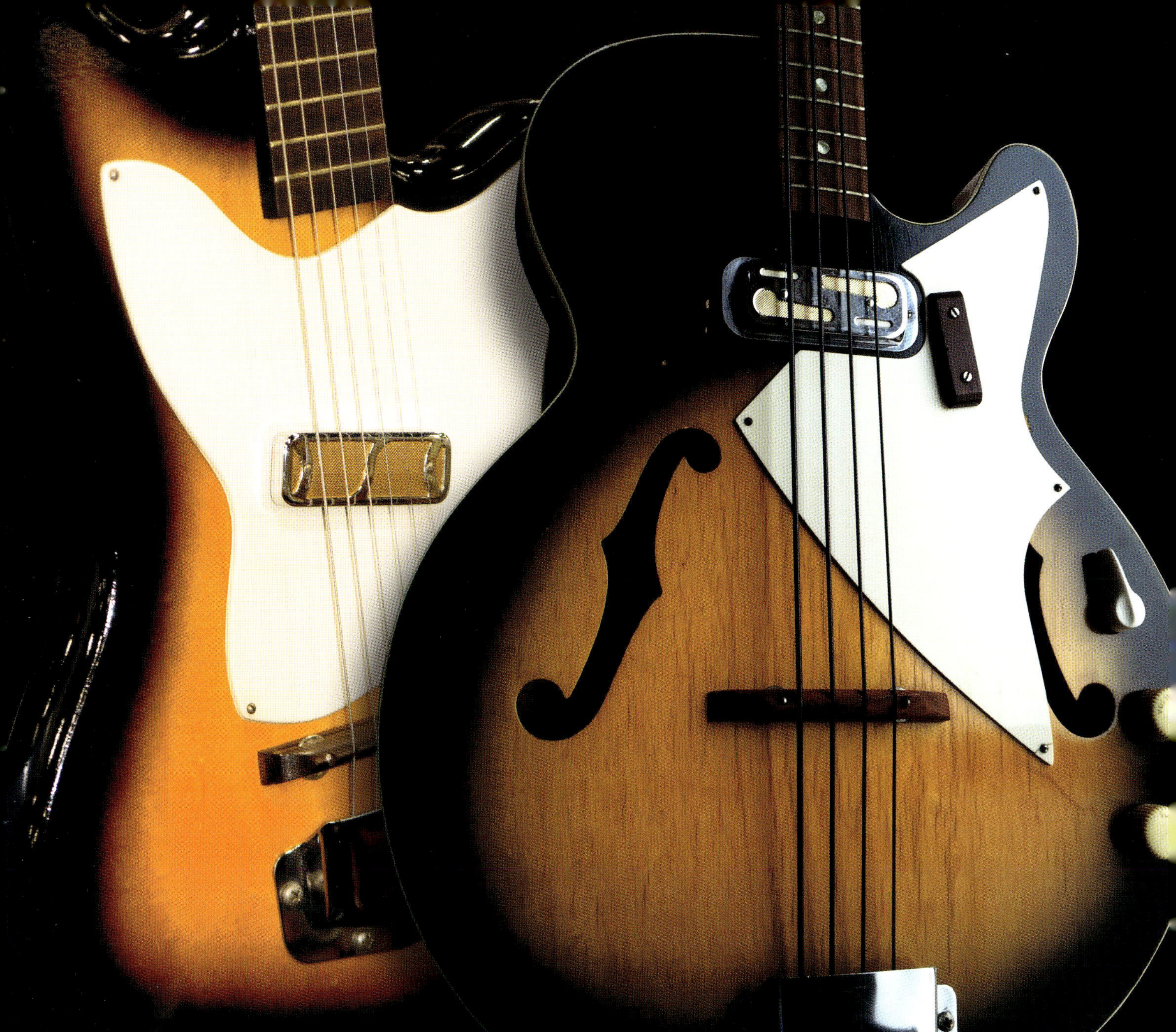

Harmony

THE PEOPLE'S GUITAR

1945–1975

RON ROTHMAN

4880 Lower Valley Road • Atglen, PA 19310

Library of Congress Control Number: 2017955188

Cover design by Justin Watinkson
Type set in Trade Gothic

ISBN: 978-0-7643-5520-2
Printed in China

Published by Schiffer Publishing, Ltd.
4880 Lower Valley Road
Atglen, PA 19310
Phone: (610) 593-1777; Fax: (610) 593-2002
E-mail: Info@schifferbooks.com
Web: www.schifferbooks.com

To Madelyn, who inspired me to call C.F. Martin & Co. when I wanted an acoustic bass, which led to my involvement in the vintage guitar business. Also to Gregory, Rebecca, and all guitar players whose first guitar was a Harmony, and the music they made.

CONTENTS

FOREWORD

Circa 1945 Harmony made stencil guitars with USA graphic and wartime wooden tailpiece.

I didn't know it at the time, but the first guitar I ever played was a Harmony. The reason I didn't know it was that it said "Silvertone" on the headstock. It was 1963, I was turning thirteen years old, and the guitar belonged to my scoutmaster. Our town, Chapel Hill, North Carolina, wasn't big enough yet to have a music store, so he had ordered it from the Sears catalog. He handed the guitar over to me along with a 45 rpm single of "Reverend Mr. Black" by the Kingston Trio, on the condition that I learn the song and play it at Boy Scout campfires. By the end of the year, my parents saw I was serious about guitar and they helped me buy one of my own, a German-made classical.

Through the 1960s, the only Harmony guitars I saw were in ads in *Sing Out!* magazine. Their slogan was "Where there's music there's Harmony," and they inserted a hand-lettered "folk" so it read, "Where there's folk music. . . ." Despite the ads, I don't remember ever seeing a Harmony in anyone's hands, and by the time I decided to step up to a quality steel-string it was 1971. I had my sight set on a Martin, Gibson, or Guild, but if I had been looking for a Harmony, I probably couldn't have found one.

It wasn't until the late 1980s, when I began researching vintage guitars, that Harmony caught my attention. I knew the company had gone under, along with Kay, in the wave of Japanese imports and that the brand had been revived on a line of cheap imports. But after seeing a few old Harmonys, my impression of Harmony as a maker of cheap, folk-era flat tops was gradually replaced by the image of a company that made guitars cheaply, to be sure, but also managed to come up with some cool designs and, surprisingly, some good-sounding guitars. I remember a black archtop electric with metal binding—an artifact from the land of Formica kitchen tables, and a Harmony Rocket—not just any Harmony Rocket but a Heathkit version, from the company that specialized in DIY electronics kits. And I remember turning the page of an old Harmony catalog and seeing the visual splash of the Colorama guitars for the first time.

This was different from nostalgia. These kitschy-cool guitars were around when I was growing up, but I hadn't been aware of them. Somehow this was a part of that era—my era—that I had completely missed.

The more I found out about Harmony the more I became intrigued with the huge number of guitars the company made. They claimed sales of 500,000 instruments in 1930, more than 100 times Martin's output. Yet I would see 100 or even 1,000 Martins from that time period before I saw a Harmony. What happened to all of them? The answer was simple. Through the years, owners of the more expensive and typically better-made Martins, Gibsons, and Fenders took care of them. Even when they didn't, they would patch them up and continue to play them; many Fenders, Gibsons, and Martins are still in use today with horrendous repairs and modifications. Not so with a Harmony. When a neckset, refret, or electronic repair cost as much or more than the guitar was worth, it got sent to the attic or thrown away.

The quality that set Harmony guitars apart from Fenders, Gibsons, and Martins—their cheapness—makes them all the more rare and special today. If you don't believe me, the proof is in my living room. Between a 1950s modern sofa and a hundred-year-old chest of drawers stands a Harmony Consolectric—a steel guitar and amp (with legs) in a box covered in tweed luggage material. The top of the box flips over to provide a handle so you can carry the rig to your gig. A year ago, when my wife and I opened our own vintage guitar store, most of our personal instruments went into the business, but not the Harmony. The Harmony has a place in our home, and there it remains.

The more expensive vintage guitars, the Fenders, Gibsons, and Martins, have received the most attention from writers and researchers. There is still much to discover about Harmony and its instruments, and for those who share my enthusiasm for finding out new things about American guitars and their place in American culture, *Harmony: The People's Guitar* is a great place to start.

Walter Carter
Spring 2014

PREFACE

I have been in the guitar business for almost twenty years as of this writing and have been to hundreds of guitar shows. Over that time many of my interests have changed. One thing, however, has remained constant. That is the pleasure I take in finding a guitar that "sounds better than it has any right to." In many cases the name on the headstock has been Harmony.

The electrics like the Rockets and Stratotones have great pickups and comfortable necks and remain playable guitars with very useful tones. No, they do not sound like Gibsons but neither do many other highly sought brands of guitars. Harmonys have a sound and a feel that are all their own and, despite their reputation as a low-end brand, they have a delightful clarity and presence.

The acoustic archtops are also very cool. Many of them have great punch and are particularly useful when recording rhythm tracks. In an odd twist, these guitars from the mid-twentieth century can breathe new life and interest in the layered guitar tracks that are a staple of modern recording in the twenty-first century.

These are, in their own way, iconic guitars from an era when the United States was gaining dominance in both music and manufacturing. The triple pickup/six knobbed Rocket in a bright red finish is the guitar equivalent of the 1957 Desoto. The same exuberant joy in life is present in both. There is neither subtlety nor restraint in either of them. They speak to a time when a real man needed lots of knobs on his guitar and fins that reached for heaven.

Ron Rothman has done the guitar public a great service by chronicling the history of the Harmony Company and the guitars they made. I was taken with the wide variety of guitars that bore the Harmony name. Flat tops, archtops, electrics, and classicals at many different levels of quality all read Harmony on the headstock. Ron looks at them all with an appreciation for their place in the vintage guitar marketplace and, more importantly, their ability to make music.

For many of us these were our first guitars and they bring back the memories of our first chords—our first handmade music. Let me say thank you, Ron, for telling their story.

Jay Pilzer
New Hope Guitars
www.guildguy.com

ACKNOWLEDGMENTS

Thanks to: Francois Demont's Harmony Database, http://harmony.demont.net/; Silvertone World website, http://www.silvertoneworld.net; Ben Chivers, www.Musicpickups.com; Jim Calhoun, Broadway Music; Jimmy Vivino; Larry Goldstein; Walter Carter; Jay Pilzer; Lonny Soury; Lorraine and Joe "Southold Slim" Sferlazza; Joe Stone; Rob Stoner; Vince Lee; Ted@DallasAlice; Les Haynie, Blue Moon Guitars; Chip Coleman; Gary and Eva, Banana Guitars; Taylor Belling; Bruce Roth, Vintage Blues Guitars; Howie Statland, Rivington Guitars; Ben and Sam Taylor, Southside Guitars; Joe Oakland; Morty Beckman, Orlando International Guitar Expo; Gary and Bonnie Burnette, Bee-3 Vintage Guitar Shows; Larry Briggs, 3 Amigo's Guitar Shows; and Matt McCabe, Saratoga Guitars. Thanks also to the countless others who had Harmony guitars to photograph and tell me about!

INTRODUCTION

In the early 1960s, I started playing music and became fascinated with the guitar, as did many of my generation. The guitars I found were those that my grandfather had in his variety and hardware store and in the catalogs from which he ordered them. Many of these were Harmony guitars and there was no better way for someone like me to develop an interest in these unique instruments. As I developed my own guitar business, as a part of the original business my grandfather started in 1918, I kept coming back to my fascination with Harmony guitars. I wanted to learn more about the instruments that had captured my interest so many years before.

While there was some information about the Harmony Guitar Company, most notably what I had read in *American Guitars: An Illustrated History* by Tom Wheeler, there was little about the guitars themselves. Most of what I was able to find out came from the guitars I had seen or owned over the years. From the acoustics I used to sell to the electrics I would find in yard sales, I've seen and owned quite a few of these instruments.

My experience actually playing Harmony guitars goes back to the early 1960s. The first guitar I owned was a Harmony acoustic and I became inspired by that student instrument.

I particularly loved the appearance of the black flat top guitar with its white pickguard that hung in the store. This was one of the more expensive guitars Grandpa Dave stocked. The last new (old stock) American-made acoustic in the store was finally sold around 1980, (an H151 acoustic). This was after I borrowed it to travel across country. I remember playing that little student size guitar, jamming on a California beach, and being impressed by how great it sounded in the open air. I still use a Harmony today for a camping guitar. The sound projection in the open air or at the beach is as good as any guitar, just as the original Harmony camp guitar might have been, when played around the campfire.

Circa 1950s Harmony made the "Lone Ranger" guitar, also available as a Supertone model 206, sold by Sears.

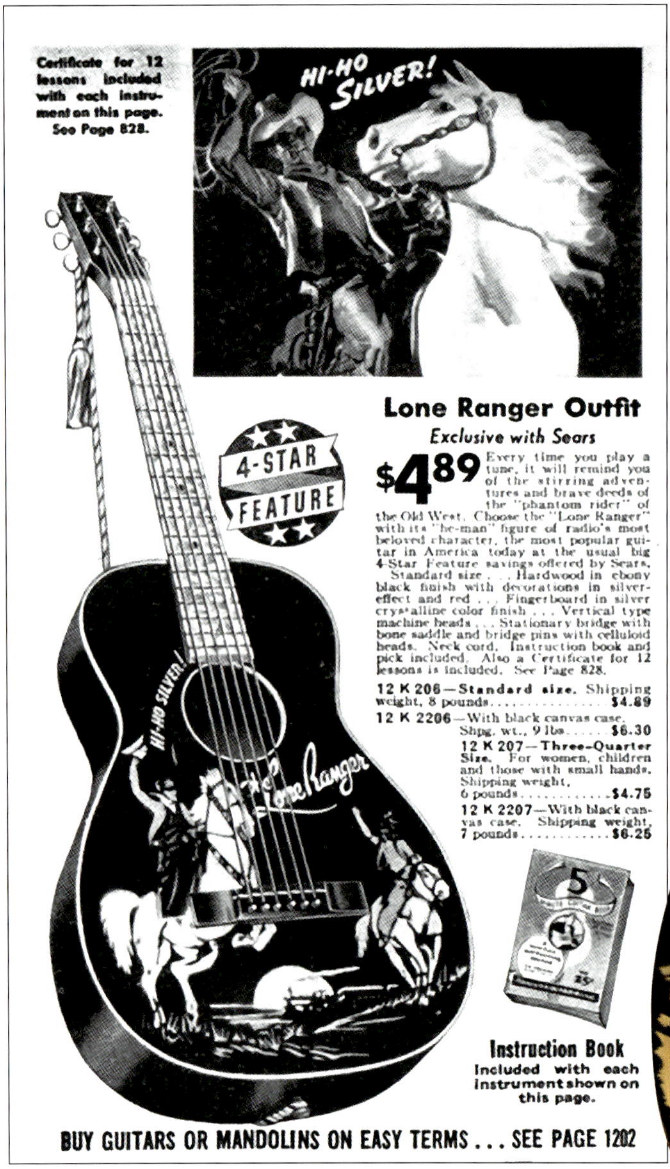
Certificate for 12 lessons included with each instrument on this page. See Page 828.
HI-HO SILVER!
4-STAR FEATURE
HI-HO SILVER!
The Lone Ranger
Lone Ranger Outfit
Exclusive with Sears
$4.89
Every time you play a tune, it will remind you of the stirring adventures and brave deeds of the "phantom rider" of the Old West. Choose the "Lone Ranger" with its "he-man" figure of radio's most beloved character, the most popular guitar in America today at the usual big 4-Star Feature savings offered by Sears.
Standard size . . . Hardwood in ebony black finish with decorations in silver-effect and red . . . Fingerboard in silver crystalline color finish . . . Vertical type machine heads . . . Stationary bridge with bone saddle and bridge pins with celluloid heads. Neck cord. Instruction book and pick included. Also a Certificate for 12 lessons is included. See Page 828.
12 K 206—Standard size. Shipping weight, 8 pounds.............$4.89
12 K 2206—With black canvas case. Shpg. wt., 9 lbs.......$6.30
12 K 207—Three-Quarter Size. For women, children and those with small hands. Shipping weight, 6 pounds.............$4.75
12 K 2207—With black canvas case. Shipping weight, 7 pounds.............$6.25
5
Instruction Book
Included with each instrument shown on this page.
BUY GUITARS OR MANDOLINS ON EASY TERMS . . . SEE PAGE 1202

Circa 1962 Harmony "Singing Cowboy" guitar, also available as a Supertone model 237.

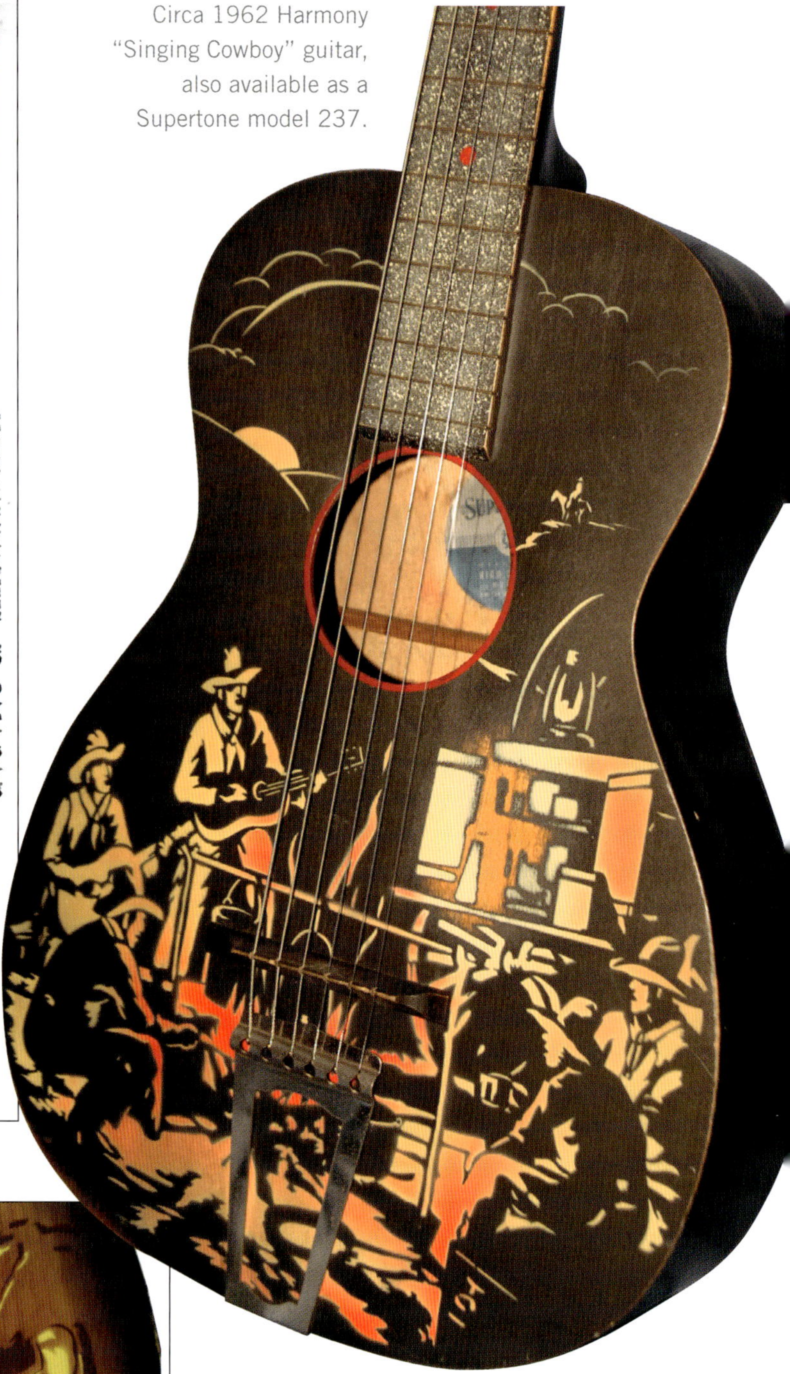

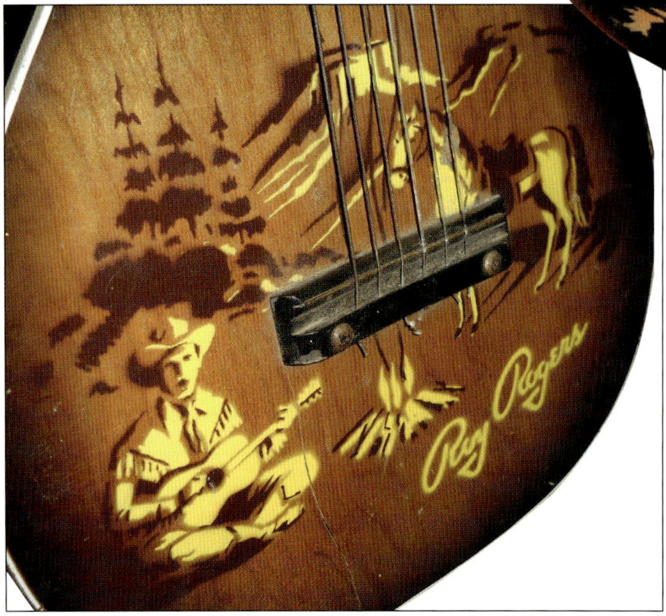
Roy Rogers

Circa 1955 Roy Rogers cowboy guitar was available as a Silvertone model 608.

As I sought out copies of the catalogs I had discarded years ago and started to acquire many guitars from those catalogs, I began researching the information about them and my dedication to Harmony guitars grew. When I realized that these vintage American-made instruments were the ones that most guitarists could afford to buy and collect, I wrote a series of articles that appeared in my own *Guitar News* and in *20th Century Guitar* magazine.

The feedback I received from around the country about these guitars motivated me to compile even more information about the Harmony Guitar Company and the guitars they produced. The first edition of my book, published in 2006, was the result.

Conversations I have had with Harmony fans at guitar shows, over the phone, and through e-mail correspondences have only confirmed that there is a never waning enthusiasm for these Chicago-made guitars. I also have found that many Harmony fans are intent on reconnecting with the guitars of their youth.

Circa 1945 Harmony ¾-size model No.939 guitar with wartime wooden tailpiece.

Circa 1940s Harmony No.1150 Faux Wood Panel acoustic guitar.

GUITARS
FRETTED INSTRUMENTS AND ACCESSORIES
HARMONY PRICE CHANGES
1973
T&D
TRUSTWORTHY
DEPENDABLE
TARG &
DINNER
INCORPORATED

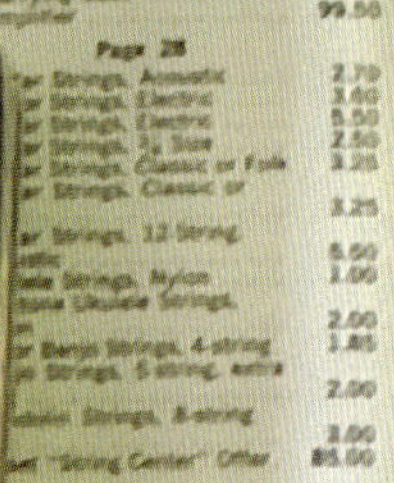

Harmony
FOR DEPENDABILITY
MADE IN AMERICA
MANUFACTURED BY
THE Harmony COMPANY
1969
Harmony
Anniversary Issue
1834-1967
CATALOG NO. 97
SINCE 1834
BRUNO
MEANS SECURITY
C. BRUNO & SON, IN

where there's music there's...

Harmony

GUITARS • ELECTRIC GUITARS • AMPLIFIERS • BANJOS • UKULELES • MANDOLINS

With this new version of my *Harmony: The People's Guitar, 1945-1975*, I am able to better explain the impact Harmony guitars have had on my generation of guitar players. At this point I can only wonder what impact Harmony guitars might have on the next generation. Whether it is a vintage Harmony or one of the recent reissues, it is the classic Harmony designs that we have come to appreciate. As the company said, "Where there's music, there's Harmony," and it really is about the music made with these guitars.

The Harmony Guitar Company was one of the more prolific manufacturers of guitars in the US. There were many guitar players inspired or frustrated when learning and playing their Harmony guitar. Whether you were one who was inspired or someone who never picked up a guitar again after your first lesson on a Harmony Stella, this book opens the door to the Harmony story that claimed to have, "touched more people and made their way into more homes, than all other American guitar makers combined."

CHAPTER 1

HARMONY: THE PEOPLE'S GUITAR

The Harmony Guitar Company was established in 1892 by Wilhelm Schultz. The Harmony name used the trademark #627412, and for decades Harmony produced countless numbers of instruments and was one of the largest manufacturers of student guitars.

Wilhelm Schultz, on the left, founder of Harmony with an unnamed factory worker and manager.

In the early part of the twentieth century, Harmony was making more mandolins than guitars. Here workers are assembling bowl back mandolins.

In a recent Reverb.com interview, Larry Goldstein reminisced: "What was even more amazing was the volume of instruments that were made like this, by hand, daily."

Workers can be seen attaching binding to guitar bodies. "In those days they used ropes and elastic bands," Goldstein says. "They would put glue on the binding and in the grooves that were cut in the guitar body and then they would wrap it with the string to hold it in place until it dried."

Even though they were competing with several other Chicago guitar companies, like Kay and Regal, Harmony still manufactured more than half the guitars sold in this country every year, for a good part of their history. As early as 1908, Harmony was already one of the largest manufacturers of mandolins, guitars, and drums in this country. They would have 25,000 instruments in production, with 10,000 completed instruments usually in stock.

Workers would use belt-driven drill presses to install tuning heads. According to Larry Goldstein, "I have to assume they're drilling for the machine heads because that would be about the only drilling you would do on a guitar. The fascinating thing to me is that everything is belt driven and how inaccurate that probably was because the speed could change so easily."

Tops are being sanded clean to prescribed thicknesses. Larry Goldstein explains in a recent Reverb.com interview, "In those days they could adjust the sanding surface—raise it or lower it—and they probably just measured it with a ruler. Even into the 1960s, Harmony never used computer numerical control in the manufacturing process," Goldstein says.

By 1915, Harmony had become the largest manufacturer of ukuleles in America, along with a variety of instruments that were in demand which included guitars, banjos, and mandolins. In 1916, the company was purchased by Sears Roebuck & Co. mainly to get a share of the ukulele market that had become a craze in this country because of the near obsession with Hawaiian music in the early part of the twentieth century.

Joe Kraus became president of Harmony in 1926 and stayed involved through the 1960s, although he would resign briefly in 1940. Charles A. "Chuck" Rubovits, who joined Harmony in 1935, would stay on when Kraus resigned and John T. Higgins was elected president of the company. Because of his expertise, Rubovitz was kept on to assist in merchandising, design, and sales. Kraus came back in January 1941, and along with C. Bruno & Co., bought out the controlling interest from Sears. After this they moved the Harmony Company to a new facility at 3633 South Racine Avenue in Chicago. Their business grew steadily and expanded through the 1960s.

Harmony was a major manufacturer of violins during the early part of the twentieth century. At that time, they were America's only large-scale violin maker. They stopped making violins for nineteen years, but started again in 1938 to fill the need of the student violinist.

The company did not sell directly to dealers; they would offer their guitars through wholesale jobber catalogs that would then sell to retailers. Many of the big mail-order catalogs carried the Harmony line, which is how most of rural America shopped at the time. Sears marketed a variety of Harmony instruments under their Silvertone label. There were a few models produced by Harmony just for the Silvertone brand, but most of the Silvertone guitars corresponded to Harmony models, except for the label and a few cosmetic details.

1
With case $199.95 cash
$9 monthly
2
3
Without case $154.95 cash
$7 monthly
4
5
Without case $84.95 cash
$5 monthly
Professional-quality features . . slimmest possible neck and strings set extra close to fingerboard to let you play your best

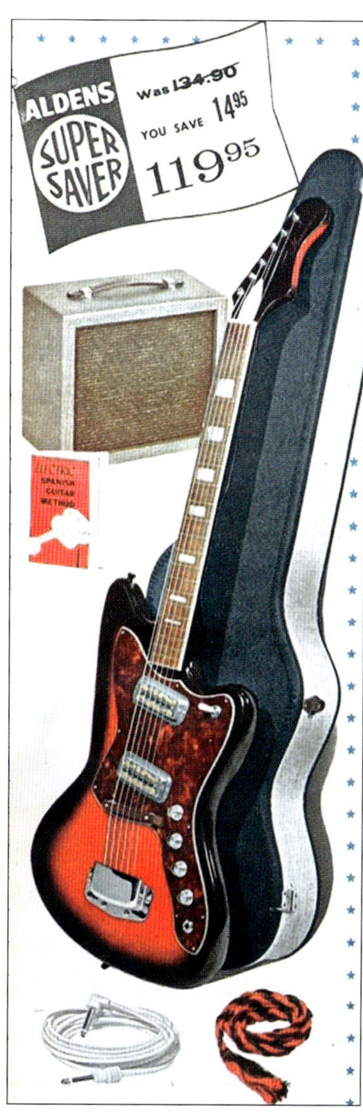
ALDENS
SUPER SAVER
Was 134.90
YOU SAVE 14.95
119.95

Circa 1971 the Harmony-made Silvertone 1453 had a body shape similar to a Rebel body, but deeper. This guitar was only available for a very short time.

Circa 1961 Silvertone 1446 was offered through the Sears catalog, and has become known as the Chris Isaak model.

Silvertones accounted for almost half of the instruments made by Harmony. The 600 series guitars were available for close to a decade.

Circa 1950s Vega E-30D electric archtop guitar with a Harmony-made body.

By the 1960s, the Silvertones accounted for almost half of the instruments made. A large number of other "house brands" were also produced by Harmony. At one point, before World War II, there were fifty-seven brand names on the same Harmony instrument. Vogue, Valencia, Johnny Marvin, Monterey, and Stella were just some of the names associated with the company. Wholesalers and private labels would use these guitars as a part of their guitar line. During the 1960s, Harmony was even producing instruments for other manufacturers like Fender and Vega. These guitars used Harmony bodies. The necks and other components were later added and put together by the guitar company that ordered them.

Stella, Airline, Stewart, Regal, and Johnny Marvin were just some of the more than fifty-seven names associated with Harmony-made instruments. If it looks like a Harmony, it probably is!

Harmony guitars would evolve in construction just like the rest of the guitar makers in this country. Through the 1940s, the instruments had clubbier necks, which tended to be "v" shaped. Some of the archtops had distinctive paddle-like headstocks. Through the 1950s, the graphics changed, as with the size of the headstock that now became smaller and simpler, which seemed to be the trend.

The better guitars might have a fancier headstock veneer, and were sometimes more colorful.

As time went on, the simpler graphics on the headstock varied from plain "Harmony" written in script, to "Harmony" and "Steel reinforced neck." Some guitars had the addition of a musical staff or note on the headstock.

Older guitars would have a wider, paddle-like headstock which became simpler over the years. A number of models were adorned with a treble clef or music note motif.

You could look inside a Harmony guitar and tell the guitars were being produced at a quick pace.

The general quality of Harmony instruments was low, lacking the attention to detail that the more expensive guitar makers were able to achieve. They would slop glue and do other things that reflected the fact that they were being mass-produced on a vast scale.

Less expensive instruments in the Harmony line would have painted fret markers, and better guitars had pearlette block inlays.

Harmony used a painted binding on their less expensive guitars. This Archtone had a multilayer painted binding with two bands until 1958, when they added a third line of faux binding.

Into the 1960s, the top of the line guitars were defined by a tortoise headstock veneer and other high end appointments such as real binding and fingerboard inlays. Cheaper models almost always had painted binding along with painted fret markers. After all, Harmony did take pride in saying they were, "The best you could buy for the money you would spend."

A tortoise headstock veneer was used on many of the better Harmony guitars.

Harmony would use fancy bridges and pickguards on both the higher end and sometimes cheaper guitar.

Looking at Harmony's guitar line, one sees how they were able to appeal to a wide range of guitarists. Their instruments varied from the less expensive Stellas to the better instruments made by Harmony that were incorporated into their Sovereign line of flat top guitars. With Sovereigns, Harmony was trying to cater to the more serious musician.

These higher-end guitars had some of the characteristics of the Gibsons that Harmony was trying to compete with, but were a less expensive alternative.

As a result of the guitar boom of the 1960s, Harmony increased its production even more and the guitars became simpler. Harmony was making an average of 1000 instruments per day during the late 1960s. Between 1945 and 1975, the Chicago firm produced approximately ten million guitars. At their peak in 1965, Harmony was grossing eleven million dollars and making half the industry's guitars, three-quarters of the ukuleles, and had a major part of the other folk instrument market. They continued to make more instruments than all other manufacturers combined.

Circa 1960s Harmony baritone uke. Fun to play!

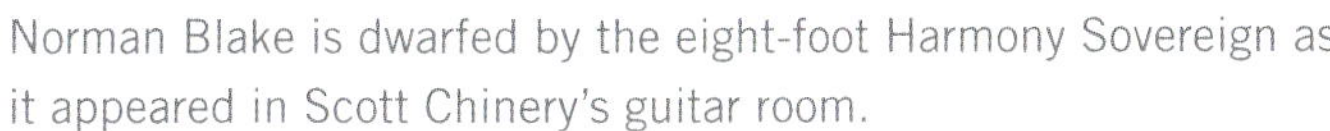

Norman Blake is dwarfed by the eight-foot Harmony Sovereign as it appeared in Scott Chinery's guitar room.

Harmony still had their own unique designs and worked on incorporating the feel of a top quality guitar. Many of the guitars from this period were rich-sounding instruments; however, you will usually find that they need the neck reset, which can be prohibitively expensive.

Their guitars were widely distributed, giving many aspiring players access to them. Harmony guitars were available to almost any business that wanted to sell them. The guitars were finding their way into many American homes and were available at a price point that just about anyone who wanted to play guitar could afford.

The Harmony Guitar Company actively promoted their instruments. They ran ads in magazines like *Sing Out!* They supplied an assortment of marketing supplies to help sell their guitars. Their ad campaigns appealed to the new generation of guitar players, and in 1970, they displayed an

70th Year Catalog

GUITARS
ELECTRIC GUITARS & AMPLIFIERS
MANDOLINS
BANJOS
UKULELES

where there's music...there's
HARMONY

eight-foot version of an H1266 Sovereign for a National Association of Music Merchandising (NAMM) show, as an advertising prop. This guitar showed the same details of its smaller counterpart. At one time, it was in the collection of the late guitar collector Scott Chinery who told me, "These Harmony Sovereigns are one of the best-valued collectible guitars.

The Harmony Guitar Company survived until the time import manufacturers took over much of the world market. The competition from the imports was one of the major forces that caused Harmony to cease production, and a real void was created. When the largest maker of student guitars in this country ceased making instruments, it helped to open the floodgate for imported guitars.

After its peak in 1964–65, Harmony's business went downhill. When Jay Kraus died in 1968, the company was taken over by a trust that decided to expand the company. They bought the distributor Targ & Dinner along with some other companies. By overextending themselves, they did not have the capital to expand and meet the demand that defined the later 1960s. They knew what had to be done, but they did not have the resources or the will to do what it would take to expand and invest even more.

Chuck Rubovitz , who had been with the company since 1935, was appointed president in 1968 and stayed with the company until 1971. When he left, Manny Kaplan was brought on as a consultant and would become Harmony's president. Kaplan tried to reimage the company by coming out with a line of better quality instruments, but it was not enough. Their indebtedness consumed them and in 1975 the factory equipment and assets were sold at auction to satisfy their creditors.

During the 1980s, the Harmony name was used on some imported guitars, but the individuality of the Harmony brand was lost. The imported guitars were becoming even more of a mass-produced instrument that was nothing more than a "cookie cutter" copy of other American designs. Maybe it was a sign of the times, or a prelude of what was to come and a reflection of the state of our country. We were finding it hard to compete pricewise with these imported, mass-produced consumer goods.

With the demise of Harmony, these great classic American-designed guitars were consigned to yard sales or otherwise ignored. There remained a core of people who would always appreciate their history and, most importantly, recognize that these were cool looking and great sounding guitars, which partially propelled the guitar culture that came to dominate music in America and much of the world.

When you look at all the imports that were coming into this country, you see all that was lost with the demise of the original Harmony Guitar Company. Harmony was, and still is, a better product than many of the imports available (up until the recent reissues) and they still are one of the more affordable American-made vintage guitars.

CHAPTER 2

SOME OF THE PARTS . . . OF MANY GUITARS

Circa 1962 Silvertone 1429 electric guitar with "silver foil" DeArmond pickups. They added a Bigsby tailpiece a year later and called it a model 1454.

The guitars made by Harmony employed numerous specifications and details. As with any manufacturer, the Harmony Guitar Company and its guitars evolved over the years. They would make different models and utilize a variety of components that were available to them. Some of these parts were developed by Harmony, while a great number were made by other manufacturers. The details, parts, names, and even model numbers would change as the years went by.

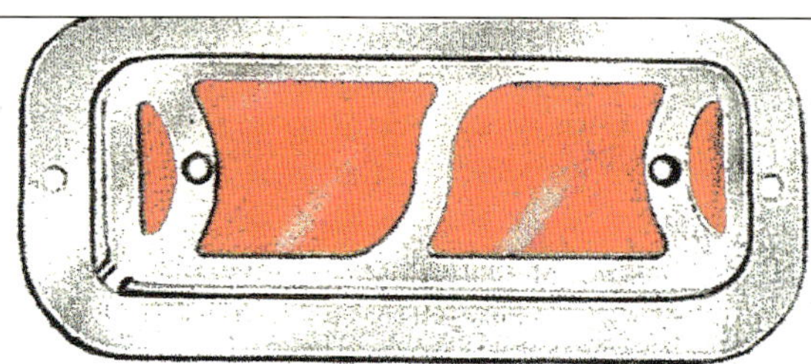

Harmony Pickups feature advanced design. Golden-Tone Indox pickups (created in cooperation with De Armond) give clearer, sharper, more responsive electric guitar sounds, have long life. Versatile circuits permit modern "big record" sound effects.

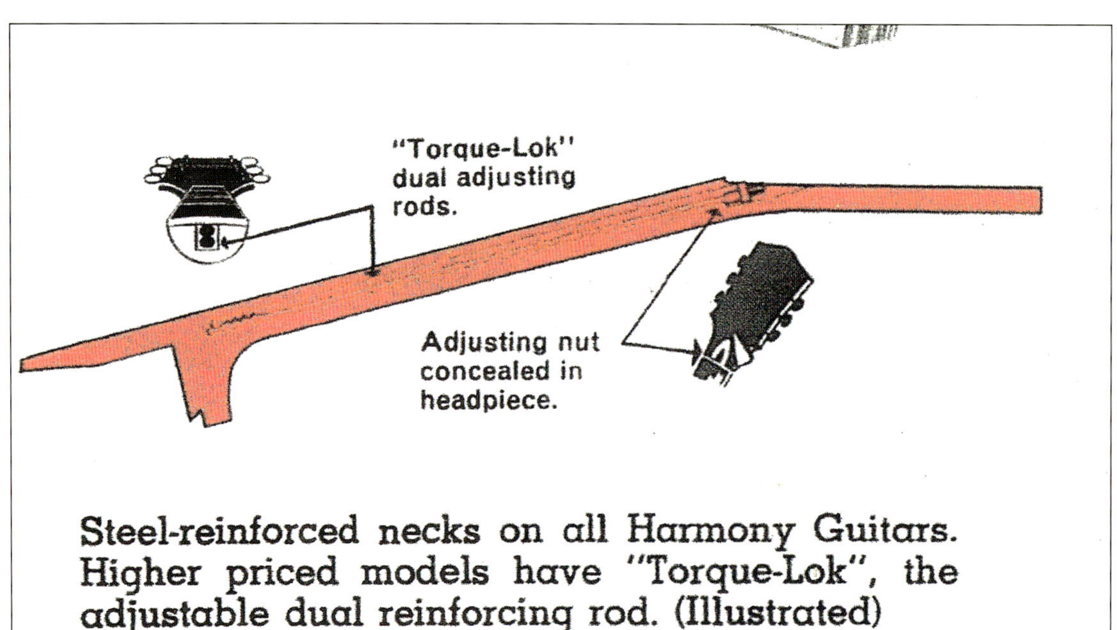

Steel-reinforced necks on all Harmony Guitars. Higher priced models have "Torque-Lok", the adjustable dual reinforcing rod. (Illustrated)

Date stamps can often be seen inside many guitars. The F-70 or F-62 will indicate the year the guitar was made.

The Francois Demont Harmony database lists close to 400 different models of Harmony guitars. This does not include models made for Silvertone and other private labels. Many guitar models were continuously in the Harmony catalogs, while a great number of them appeared for only a short period of time. Some of the model numbers were just variations of existing guitars. Some guitars had the same model number but were totally different guitars. By the mid 1970s, it appeared that many guitar models were just being renumbered. The Targ & Dinner wholesale catalog added prefix numbers, creating a whole new set of model designations. Documenting the many different model designations is arduous as there are so many model numbers.

DeArmond would have a date printed on the pickup to show the date of manufacture.

Many of the guitars made by Harmony in the 1960s would incorporate an HXXX in the serial number stamped inside the guitar. This was one of the more commonly seen model designation systems found on Harmony guitars. The numbers after the H would indicate the model. The numbers before the H would indicate a sequence number. The batch number that preceded the model was reset for each run and did not indicate the date the guitars were produced. A variety of guitars have smaller numbers such as S-62, F-66, and FW-59 stamped inside the guitar along with, or without, "Made in the USA." This number indicates the year of manufacture, but it doesn't appear in all guitars. The F indicated the fall manufacturing run for the holiday season. The S indicated they were being made for the summer run. Or, as I was told by an old factory worker, "F-First and S-Second factory run," still, for some reason, corresponding to fall and spring. While this system was used in the 1960s, earlier catalogs would show models listed without the "H" designation (i.e., No.920.) The numbering system used by Harmony, while confusing, would usually indicate the model number in some form, when it was visible. There was a core group of models consistently used through the 1960s; these will be the focus of the guitars that will be discussed in this book.

While many of the model numbers in the later 1960s have the HXXX, some of the electrics can only be accurately dated by the date stamp on the DeArmond pickups. This was a manufacturer's number by Rowe Industries, and can be an accurate way of dating these guitars.

Circa 1950s Harmony H50 with an earlier, no pole Gibson-made P-13 pickup.

This DeArmond chrome soap bar pickup, also referred to as the "Hershey Bar" pickup, was used on several of the earlier Harmony models. This basic model had an extended plate for surface mounting or installing the pickguard.

Harmony was a company that would utilize parts that came from an assortment of manufacturers for their guitars. One of the things that made the electric guitars stand out from the other guitar makers were the different pickups they chose to use. Harmony changed the pickups they used as time went on, using specific pickups that would define different models. The first Spanish electric guitars had a Gibson-made P-13 pickup, the same one that had been used with Harmony's early lap steel guitars. These pickups were a single coil, "soap bar" style pickup. They would have either adjustable screw, square non-adjustable poles, or blade (no poles) and were used on many of the early full bodied archtops. Also used on the Espanadas, Roy Smecks, and full-size archtop guitars, P-13 pickups were a big part of establishing the Harmony sound.

The first DeArmond pickup to be introduced and used by Harmony was the "Hershey Bar" pickup. These chrome clad, single coil pickups were found with different types of mounting plates and were used on a variety of Harmony guitars including the early Hollywoods and Rivieras. They were also found on the early H44 Stratotones. A variation of this was used on the H88 Stratotone when a raised bar was riveted to the body of the pickup. It was purely ornamental and did not affect the sound.

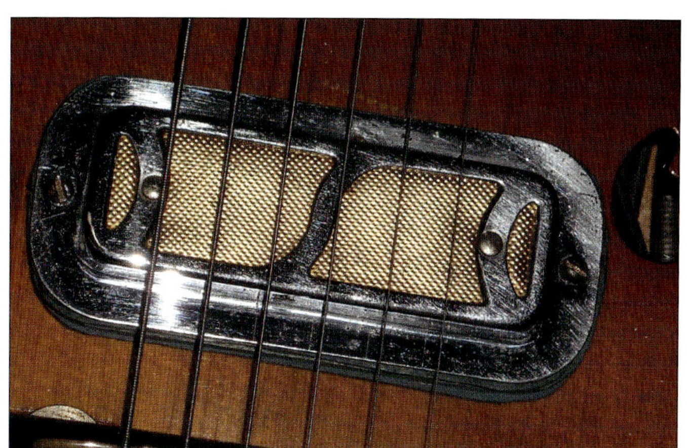

Harmony's "S-grill," gold foil DeArmond pickup was used on many models during the 1960s and was available as a soap bar or with an attached, chrome bezel.

By the early 1960s, Harmony was using the DeArmond "Golden-Tone" foil face pickup on a number of their guitars. These pickups would be used with various grills for different guitars. The DeArmond "S" Grill over the gold foil pickups were used on guitars like the earlier Rockets and later Hollywoods. The same pickups were also used on Harmony-made Silvertone guitars and had a "Diamond" Grill over a silver foil face. Similar pickups were used on Montgomery Ward's Roy Smeck guitars, which had a different diamond pattern for the front of the pickup. When incorporated with a blender control (i.e., the H49 Stratotone and H41 Hollywood), they made for some great sounding guitars and allowed for a variety of tones.

Francois Demont refers to the different "families" of Harmony guitars and this is a good way of organizing the types of guitars that were produced by Harmony. While this book pretty much follows that method of organization, there may be a number of models that will be overlooked because they are slight variations of other models. I try to touch on most of the various styles of guitars, taking into account many different models, while talking about specific guitars.

The sum of the parts makes up the whole guitar. The guitars changed over the years, as did the parts, but until the mid 1970s, Harmony would use components that would be chosen to help create and establish their unique identity.

CHAPTER 3

STELLAS TO SOVEREIGNS: HARMONY FLAT TOPS, 1950–1973

Circa 1950s Harmony H929 Stella with its faux grained top. "Excellent for students or home playing. Nicely highlighted and grained; white striping on top edge and sound hole."

The Silvertone 600 series guitar was similar to a Harmony H931 and had a "Pinless type ebonized maple bridge, firmly secured in place."

We've all them and we've all loved them. The number of baby boomers who started guitar lessons on a Harmony student guitar was huge. They were affordable and could be quite playable. The student guitars made by the Harmony Guitar Company of Chicago were readily available to the masses. Most music stores carried them along with a whole assortment of mail-order catalogs that also sold Harmonys. Sears, who owned the Harmony Company for a period of time, would make these guitars available via mail order to their customers under the Silvertone label. This made the Harmony manufactured Silvertone 600 series acoustic guitar an equally popular choice for a beginner.

There were an assortment of Stella guitars with similar features. The model number might change, color might be a little different, but overall they were the same guitar. One variation would be the type of tailpiece and bridge used.

While some of the earlier guitars had only "Stella" on the headstock, Harmony later added the "Harmony" name under the Stella name.

Circa 1960s Harmony H929 Stella, a very popular model with many variations produced and sold under assorted brand names. The white plastic pickguard was added in 1961.

Circa 1950/60s Stella model H928 in the "Ivory burst" faux grain top. "All birch, floating bridge and metal tailpiece."

Circa 1950s Harmony H929 Stella with its faux grained top. "Standard Size-Mahogany shaded finish guitar."

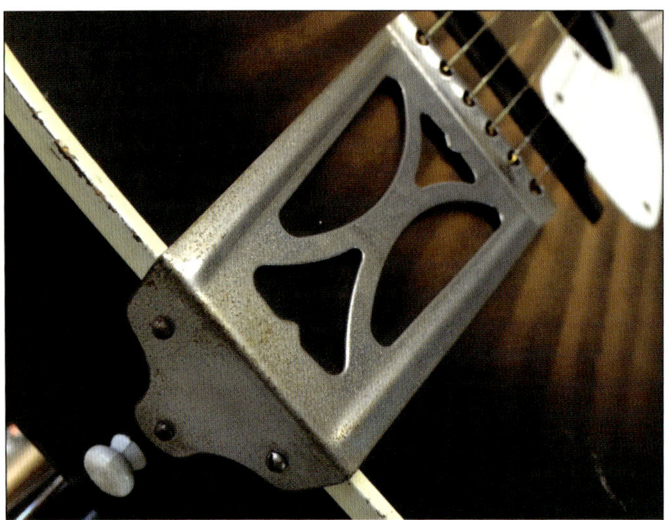

Circa 1961 Harmony H929 Stella used a pressed metal tailpiece with floating bridge.

Most of the Harmony guitars one sees are from the 1960s, as a result of the guitar boom that took place when the Beatles took America by storm. Harmony offered a selection of student models at that time. The No.1141 may have had a little different shape from the traditional small bodied Stellas, but many models were just variations of the H929. By the late 1960s, Harmony offered a better quality Stella guitar. The H942 natural Grand Concert size guitar had a "simulated marquetry ring" at the sound hole and was an attractive upgrade from the H929. There was the added feature of a screwed-down bridge on these Stella guitars.

"Perfection," was Harmony's goal throughout its history. Their claim to have sold "more stringed instruments than all other makers in America combined—and thus created thousands of friends for Harmony all over the world" held true. Harmony made their guitars available to the masses so the student had an affordable option. These Stella instruments were a guitar that most beginners could afford to own. They still remain one of the more affordable American vintage guitars to this day.

No. TG1201

No. 162

No. 165

U
21

Made in America

Harmony Flat Top

YOUNG PEOPLE particularly look to the "flat top" to capture the romance of traditional folk and Country and Western music, as well as the contemporary mode of self-expression in song. Harmony presents a wide selection for every taste and budget.

No. 1260. Harmony Sovereign — Jumbo Model—The rich deep sustained bass and clear treble tones so desirable for folk and Country and Western music are "built-in" this specially designed Sovereign Jumbo model. The large deep body has selected mahogany back and sides, resonant spruce top, white edge bindings, with inlays. The Torque-Lok reinforced mahogany "Slim-Line" neck, with ovalled rosewood fingerboard, makes chording and playing fast and easy. Beautifully highly polished. Size 16 x 4 [illegible]/16 x 40¾ in. . . .

No. C-550—Carrying Case . . . .

No. 1265. Harmony Sovereign DeLuxe Jumbo Model—For outstanding appearance and performance. A professional type addition to the famous family of Sovereign quality guitars. Made of carefully selected materials—resonant mahoganies and spruce. Constructed to emphasize sustained deep bass and brilliant treble tone quality. Special headpiece design, engraved. Out-size pickguard. Rich appearing bridge with adjustable saddle. Richly shaded and polished, in an eye-appealing sunburst finish. Size 16 x 4 [illegible]/16 x 41½ in. . . . . .

No. C-551—Carrying Case . . . .

No. 1260

No. 1265

No. 1203

1961

Harmony FLAT TOP GUITARS

"SLIM LINE" Neck With TORQUE-LOK Reinforcing Rod

HARMONY SOVEREIGN — WESTERN SPECIAL

Full toned, responsive for solo playing. Has "Slim Line" neck with Torque-Lok reinforcing rod—fast, easy to finger for modern guitar performance. Polished natural finish selected spruce top, inlaid at soundhole and edge with pin lines. Back, frame, and neck are of fine polished mahogany. Ovaled rosewood fingerboard. Pinless type rosewood bridge. Size 15⅛x40 in.

No. 1203 .... Each **$62.50**

"SLIM LINE" Neck With TORQUE-LOK Reinforcing Rod

No. 1203 $62.50

No. 1260 $72.50

for Folk and Western MUSIC

HARMONY SOVEREIGN — NEW JUMBO

The rich deep sustained bass and clear treble tones so desirable for Western and folk music are "built-in" this specially designed Sovereign Jumbo model. The large deep body has selected mahogany back and sides, resonant spruce top, shell edge bindings, and inlays. The Torque-Lok reinforced mahogany "Slim-Line" neck, with ovalled rosewood fingerboard, makes chording and playing fast and easy. Beautifully finished, polished.

No. 1260 .... Each **$72.50**

Dimensions
Width, below bridge — 16 in.
Width, at shoulder — 11-3/4 in.
Depth of body — 4-5/16 in.
Length all-over — 40-1/4 in.

There was much more to Harmony's flat top guitars than their Stella line. Of the thousands of kids who started playing guitar, some were fortunate enough to step up to the better made, or "professional" line of guitars. Harmony was the most diverse with the different models they offered; they had to keep up with the demand of what was becoming a cult phenomenon. The flat top guitar had transcended the country music genre, and with the birth of the folk music revolution, the flat top was here to stay.

Circa 1960s Harmony Sovereign H1260 was the flagship of the Harmony acoustic line.

Circa 1967 Harmony H1265 Deluxe Sovereign with its asymmetrical "Africa" double pickguard appeared in the catalog for only a short time.

In 1950, Harmony offered three flat tops and three Stella guitars. By the 1970s, they responded to the growing popularity of the flat top acoustic guitar and manufactured more than twenty different flat tops. While Harmony still offered acoustic archtop guitars, there were few self-respecting "folkies" that would be caught playing one. By 1961, Harmony had begun to establish different models in its line. The Jumbo Sovereign, Model No.1260, along with the smaller Model No.1203, were their better quality guitars and they would continue in their catalog in some variation. The 1971 catalog showed an assortment of upgraded Sovereigns and included the H1266 and black H1264, with double pickguards.

Circa 1970 Harmony H1266 Deluxe Sovereign with mirrored pickguard. "A professional type addition to the famous family of Sovereign quality guitars."

This circa 1969 Harmony H162 acoustic guitar was a very popular model that was in production for over thirty years.

Circa 1974 Harmony H6364 Sovereign. "Jet black with contrasting inlaid purfling, white binding, and inlays on edges."

Circa 1960s Harmony H165 all mahogany guitar. "Resonant tone quality for solo playing or accompaniment of songs."

Their other Grand Concert size guitars, in 1962, were listed in the catalog as a mahogany top, model No.165, and a spruce top, model No.162 which were their less expensive models. All of these guitars were solid wood and consistently available from Harmony in some version, over the years.

HARMONY STUDIO SPECIAL

Best Beginners or "Loaner" Guitar

- Special Short Scale—Thin Neck
- Less Space Between Frets—Makes fingering easier for big or little fingers.
- Reduced Depth Body—But full size for tone.
- Comfortable to hold.
- Economical to Maintain—Celluloid edges — Celluloid Pickguard — Durable Finish.

Helps teachers and beginners many ways. Short (¾ size) scale eases finger placement and chord formation for students of all ages. Standard size thinner body is comfortable to hold, has full tone. Durable hardwood construction and finish, genuine celluloid bindings and pickguard, bone nut, bolted-on pinless bridge, permit repeated "loaning" with minimum maintenance.

No. 150—Size 13⅛x34¼ in. Each **$32.50**

P
16

The Harmony Studio Specials were noted in the catalog as being "Best for the beginners or 'loaner' guitar."

One of the more common Harmony models was the H162. Prior to 1957, the guitar had a more pronounced "hour glass" design.

Circa 1970 Harmony H151 with its stenciled rosette and pickguard. "Thin Neck, Special Short Scale – Less Space Between Frets – Makes fingering easier for big or little fingers."

Circa 1970s Harmony H4101 tenor guitar. At this time Harmony was starting to use paper labels in their guitars.

Toward the end of USA Harmony, they tried to offer better guitars that were a departure from their typical student guitars for which they had come to be known. They introduced their Regal line of guitars, and what would be a better "X" braced guitar as part of their Opus line of guitars.

Harmony had their fair share of the student guitar market. They had price points for all incomes and levels of guitar players. Their focus was on the beginner market, but they did try to offer an instrument that might appeal to the more advanced or professional player. They had the goods, but just weren't able to survive the 1970s.

Circa 1960s Silvertone 600 series was equally as popular as the Harmony Stella guitar.

H6659. Impressive Dreadnought Model—big, deep bodied, and resonant—for folk or country-and-western music. Moves you right into that big guitar sound—at a moderate price. Has the new adjustable reinforced narrow neck and fingerboard (1¾" at nut, 2⅛" at soundhole.) Top is spruce grained; back, sides, and neck in dark rosewood color. Simulated inlay rings around soundhole. Ebonized ovalled fingerboard with 6 inlaid position markers. Ebonized adjustable pin bridge. Size 4½ x 16 x 40⅜ in. $59.95
H0660. Carrying Case. $16.00

H6364. Rich, Spectacular, Jet Black Sovereign Folk Guitar in Grand Concert Size. With beautiful contrasting inlaid rings around soundhole, white bindings and inlays on body edges. Solid spruce top, hardwood back, sides and neck—all highly polished. Adjustable, reinforced "Slim-Line" neck, ovalled rosewood fingerboard with 6 inlaid position dots and bound edges. Adjustable rosewood pin bridge. Size 15⅜ x 39 in. $89.95

H6303. Harmony Sovereign Grand Concert Model, embodying the perfection of tone quality that has made it one of the most popular over the years. Selected, natural solid spruce top, highly polished. Inlaid at soundhole and bound edges. Polished mahogany back, sides and neck. Adjustable reinforced "Slim-Line" neck for fast, easy fingering. Ovalled rosewood fingerboard. Pinless rosewood bridge. Size 15⅜ x 40 in. $109.95

H6382. Deluxe Grand Concert Size Folk Guitar with magnificent tone quality. Finest natural solid spruce top from our selection of choice spruce; mahogany back, sides and the **new thin narrow,** adjustable reinforced neck in dark rosewood finish. Brilliantly polished. Adjustable rosewood pin bridge, and fingerboard (1¾" at nut, 2⅛" at soundhole) with edge bindings and 7 inlaid position dots. Bindings and inlays on body edges and around soundhole. Individual covered tuning keys, with pearlized buttons. Size 15⅜ x 40 in. $119.95
H0315. Carrying Case for Grand Concert Size Guitars. $15.50

5

Opposite, bottom right: Circa 1960s Harmony H181/H180 guitar that had the less common six on a side tuners, along with a fancy bridge and stenciled pickguard. *Photo courtesy of Lonnie Soury*

CHAPTER 4

HARMONY ACOUSTIC ARCHTOP GUITARS

Circa 1961 Harmony H1214 Archtone with a "blonde" ivory enamel finish that has a grained effect.

Circa 1960s Harmony Monterey Leader with its faux grained top. These Monterey guitars were Harmony's more popular archtop guitar which was produced for more than thirty years.

Harmony

ARCHED

GUITARS

1213

1214

1215

TENOR GUITAR
4-string model, similar to No. 1215 Guitar
No. TG1215 Ea. $27.50

HARMONY AUDITORIUM MODEL
Arched top and back, birch, with F-holes, in a pleasing brown mahogany shaded and highlighted finish. White striped edges. Ovaled hard maple fingerboard, grained to resemble rosewood. Celluloid guard-plate, on bracket; adjustable bridge.
No. 1213........ Each $27.50

HARMONY AUDITORIUM MODEL
Attractive "blonde" ivory enamel finish with grained effect. Black striped edges and pin line. Fully arched top and back, birch construction. Ovaled fingerboard. Black guardplate, on nickel plated bracket. Adjustable bridge. Plated tailpiece.
No. 1214........ Each $27.50

HARMONY AUDITORIUM MODEL
Arched top and back, birch, with F-holes, in a glossy brown mahogany shaded and grained finish. White striped edges. Ovaled hard maple fingerboard, grained to resemble rosewood. Celluloid guardplate, on bracket; adjustable bridge.
No. 1215........ Each $27.50

When you look through the old catalogs from the 1960s, you will see a great number of archtops. It would appear that Harmony must have had a large customer base for the "F" hole guitar. The number of different models made by Harmony showed how there must have been a great calling for these archtop guitars. The different models, by the late 1960s, were as diverse as the kinds of people who were to play them and at price points they could afford to pay.

Circa 1945 Harmony H950 Monterey with its wartime wood tailpiece, one of their most popular archtops.

1950s Harmony-made Sonata house brand.

Budget priced, these Harmony H1213 Archtone guitars had a multilayer painted binding, missing the pickguard.

No. H950
$69.50
Also Tenor Model

FAMOUS
Harmony
MONTEREY
LEADER
950

Circa 1950 Harmony H1327 Monterey. This Grand Auditorium version had herringbone binding.

No. H950
$69.50
Also Tenor Model

Circa 1960s Harmony Monterey HTG950 four string tenor guitar matched the No.950 six string model.

There were several archtop models that Harmony consistently produced as part of their diverse selection of instruments. The Harmony Master H945 was a birch guitar that was celluloid bound and had painted block fingerboard position markers. The long running H950 Monterey Leader and Broadway H954 would offer a decent option, at an affordable price. There was the H1310 "top of the line" guitar, which had a solid arched spruce top that was referred to in the catalog as the "Brilliant Cutaway" model. Harmony would also continue to produce non-cutaway archtop models, which were either designated as a Monterey, Montclair, or Patrician, model names that survived in the Harmony catalog from the 1940s. These model names were used for their "Professional" arched guitars and the same names would be used on various Harmony archtop models over the years.

Circa 1971 Harmony H1310 acoustic archtop guitar. "Brilliant cutaway guitars – with 'Slim Line' Torque-Lok necks."

Budget priced and fun to play, some of these archtops made their way into the attics and under the beds of countless numbers of American homes. Pushed there by the demand for flat tops during the guitar boom that took place during the 1960s, these archtop guitars faded away into the woodwork. The more serious jazz player was looking for better quality and the everyday player just wasn't playing this style of guitar any longer. Most guitar makers just didn't see the demand for archtops at this time. It seems Harmony was still able to appreciate the limited demand for archtop guitars, and did continue to produce them.

Circa 1940s Harmony Patrician with wartime wood tailpiece. A guitar that had been well played.

1954

Harmony

CREMONA

CARVED TOP CUTAWAY MODEL GUITAR

Here is Harmony's advanced instrument for the exacting player who seeks an acoustical guitar with the finest in tone quality, design, and craftsmanship. The resonant tonal value of a top carved and hand-finished from a solid block of carefully selected fine-grained spruce is combined with modern functional design permitting a smooth sweep of the left hand from the neck into the "cutaway" for maximum ease in fingering to the 20th fret.

1302

1301

SUNBURST FINISH. Grand Auditorium size. Carefully graduated carved spruce top. Selected maple back and sides. Modern highly polished finish, beautifully highlighted and shaded in sunburst effect. Rosewood headpiece and ovalled fingerboard inlaid with genuine mother-of-pearl. Edges bound with heavy celluloid. Top edge has wide inlays. Heavy Lucite pickguard. Professional type frets. Individual tuning units, metal buttons.
No. 1301 ....Each **$125.00**

BLOND FINISH. Companion model to No. 1301. Highly polished natural finish. Heavy edge bindings, wide contrasting inlays on top edge. Rosewood adjustable bridge, bone saddle. Compensating tailpiece.
No. 1302 ....Each **$135.00**

Harmony CUTAWAYS

Harmony's fine new precision-built Cutaway model. The smooth sweep from neck into the gracefully shaped Cutaway enables the player to finger to the 20th fret with great ease. Grand Auditorium size, arched maple back, and selected quality arched spruce top. Heavy edge bindings and inlays. Rosewood headpiece and fingerboard, with pearlette inlays. Individual tuning units. Heavy Lucite pick-guard. Skillfully shaded highly polished modern lasting finish. An instrument designed for beauty and musicianship.
No. 1310 ....Each **$87.50**

1310

1311

Blond, companion model to No. 1310. Black and white inlays. Pearlette inlaid rosewood headpiece and fingerboard. Highly polished blond finish.
No. 1311 ....Each **$92.50**

Circa 1960s Harmony H945 Master acoustic archtop guitar. "For the advancing player, the Master model offers tone quality, easy playing, at a moderate price."

Circa 1952 Harmony H1457 Grand Auditorium blonde model archtop.

CHAPTER 5

HARMONY HOLLYWOOD AND THE SPANISH ELECTRIC ARCHTOP GUITARS

Circa 1950s Harmony H50 "Grand Auditorium" size guitar utilized a single "Tone-Emphasizer" pickup. One of the first Harmony electric guitars.

During the 1950s, the world saw the electric archtop guitar come into popularity with guitar players. In their catalog, Harmony referred to the archtop as a Spanish electric guitar. The archtop had been the favored style of guitar, but now as electronics, pickups, and amplifiers were being developed, the need for a Spanish electric guitar was necessitated and pickups were being added to these archtop guitars.

SPANISH ELECTRIC

GUITARS

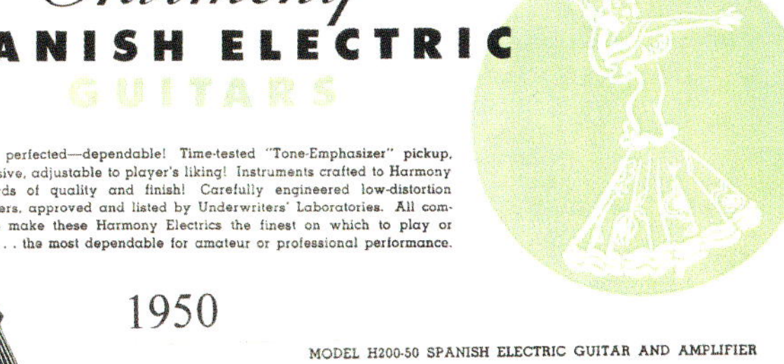

Highly perfected—dependable! Time-tested "Tone-Emphasizer" pickup, responsive, adjustable to player's liking! Instruments crafted to Harmony standards of quality and finish! Carefully engineered low-distortion amplifiers, approved and listed by Underwriters' Laboratories. All combine to make these Harmony Electrics the finest on which to play or teach . . . the most dependable for amateur or professional performance.

1950

MODEL H200-50 SPANISH ELECTRIC GUITAR AND AMPLIFIER

The guitar is Grand Auditorium size, in rich two-tone sunburst polished finish. Celluloid bound and inlaid. Engraved headpiece. Rosewood fingerboard and bridge. Individual tuning keys. Built-in Spanish type "Tone-Emphasizer" pickup, adjustable to players' liking. Has volume and tone control.

5 tube amplifier, excellent tone, high volume. 10 to 14 watts output at minimum distortion. 3 inputs, including microphone. 3 controls for volume and tone. 10" dynamic speaker. Handsome two-tone cabinet, balanced for easy carrying. Underwriters' Laboratories approved.

No.		
H200-50	Guitar and Amplifier..	$172.00†
H200	Amplifier only..	89.50†
H50	Guitar only	82.50†
C50	Guitar Carrying Case, extra	12.00†

MODEL H195-51 SPANISH ELECTRIC GUITAR AND AMPLIFIER

Efficient, full toned, at a moderate price. Guitar is Auditorium size, arched, pleasingly shaded, highly polished. "Tone-Emphasizer" pickup, adjustable, with volume and tone controls.

4 tube amplifier, reproduces with high fidelity. 8 watt output at low distortion. Inputs for 2 instruments, or instrument and microphone; separate volume controls. 8" dynamic speaker. Sturdy cabinet in two-tone leatherette, piped; metal grill. Inspected and listed by Underwriters' Laboratories.

No.		
H195-51	Guitar and Amplifier..	$130.00†
H195	Amplifier only	70.00†
H51	Guitar only	60.00†
C51	Guitar Carrying Case, extra..	11.00†

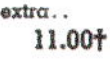

3

Harmony

RIVIERA

ELECTRIC SPANISH GUITAR

Bright Chrome-like "HARMOMETAL" Binding on Edges

1955

"Harmometal" means the newest in styling, the most perfect protection, the most all-around beauty. Super Auditorium size Arched model. Rich Pacific Blue Colorama finish with Dawn Blue panel. "Balanced tone" magnetic pickup with tone and volume control and 8 ft. cord.

No. H41 Riviera Guitar **$57.50**

No. C39 Carrying Case, extra **$11.00**

Circa 1951 Harmony H50 Spanish electric guitar. Early models (pre-50) had "f"-holes in one part, not segmented. *Jay Pilzer photo*

Circa 1940s Harmony H50, natural finish with wrap around pickguard and was one of the earlier Harmony Spanish electric guitars.

Harmony came out with the H50 Archtop as their version of the Gibson ES-125 to fit the demand of the music at this time and was one of Harmony's first electric guitars. The non-cutaway, single pickup guitar used their "Tone-Emphasizer" pickup, like the ones they had been using on some of their steel guitars. The Gibson-made P-13 pickup added to, and helped define, the "Harmony Sound" and was one of the first pickups to be used by Harmony. The catalog claimed them to be "Designed for easy response and full rich tone."

Harmony HOLLYWOOD Colorama

ELECTRIC SPANISH GUITARS

An outstanding combination of value and eye appeal for the advancing player who wants to practice and perform on a moderately priced electric.

Arched model — Super Auditorium size — hardwood construction — ovalled fingerboard — adjustable bridge. Practical responsive magnetic pickup, with volume control and 8 ft. cord.

Length 40½ in.
Width 15¾ in.

No. H37

No. H38

Choice of 2 finishes:
No. H37 Guitar, Metallic gold with Black panel............$49.50

No. H38 Guitar, Black with Metallic gold panel............$49.50

No. C39 Carrying Case, extra...$11.00

Circa 1955 Harmony Hollywood H37 electric archtop guitar. This example has had the fixed cord shortened and repaired.

Circa 1962 Harmony H37 gold and black Hollywood with single DeArmond pickup.

No. H39

No. H41

The Harmony Hollywood was one of the only non-cutaway Spanish electric archtop guitars to survive, and it lasted in Harmony's catalog until about 1967. Maybe it had to do with the changing times or blinding glamour of Hollywood that appealed to the guitar buyer. Both the single and double pickup with blender switch, were in their catalogs through the 1960s, but this style of guitar gave way to the popularity of the flat top and demand for thinner electric archtops with cutaways. The Rockets, Meteors, and higher end guitars would slowly replace these full depth guitars that blazed the trail for the Harmony electrics that were to come.

Circa 1960s Harmony H39 Hollywood with single DeArmond pickup with body mounted controls.

Circa 1960s Harmony H41 Hollywood had two DeArmond pickups and utilized a blender switch for a variety of sounds.

CHAPTER 6

HARMONY STRATOTONE AND THE SOLID BODY ELECTRIC GUITARS

Circa 1960s Aldens version of an H45 Mars with single "Hershey Bar" pickup with an ornamental dimpled center strip that did not affect the sound. It was not until after 1962 that Harmony added the "Atomic" logo to the pickguard. This example has a black, sparkle finish.

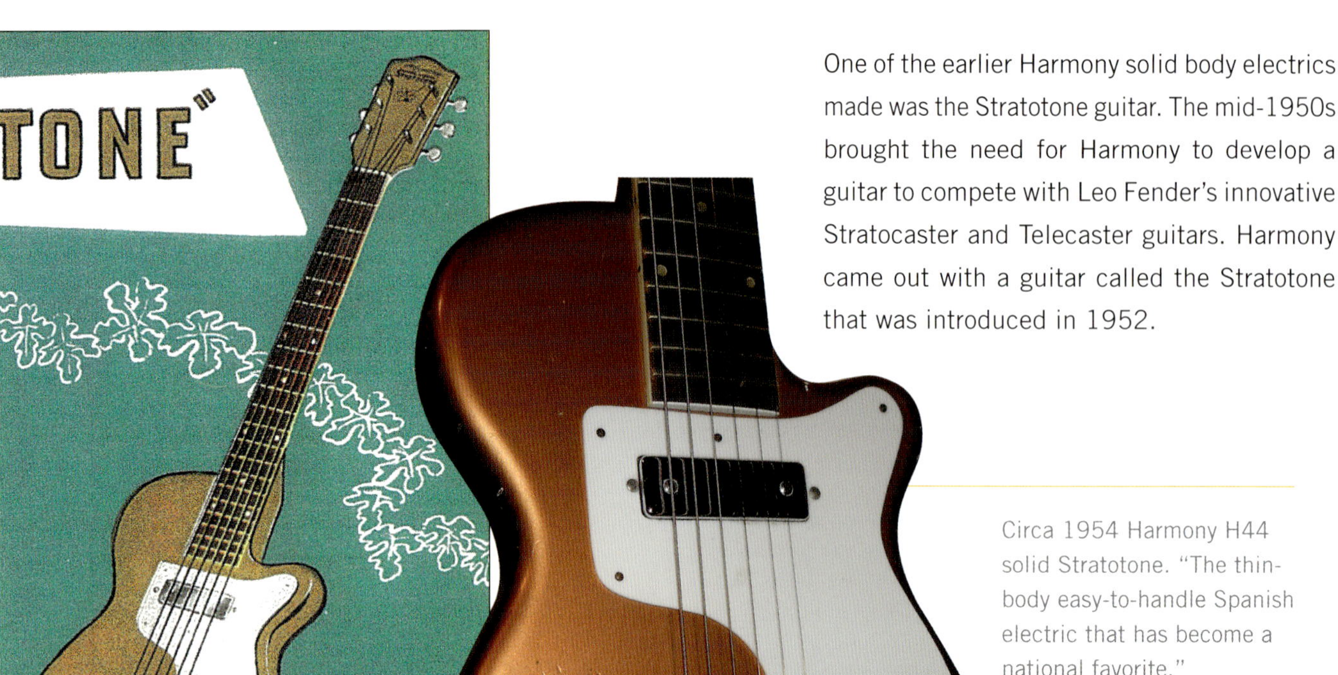

One of the earlier Harmony solid body electrics made was the Stratotone guitar. The mid-1950s brought the need for Harmony to develop a guitar to compete with Leo Fender's innovative Stratocaster and Telecaster guitars. Harmony came out with a guitar called the Stratotone that was introduced in 1952.

Circa 1954 Harmony H44 solid Stratotone. "The thin-body easy-to-handle Spanish electric that has become a national favorite."

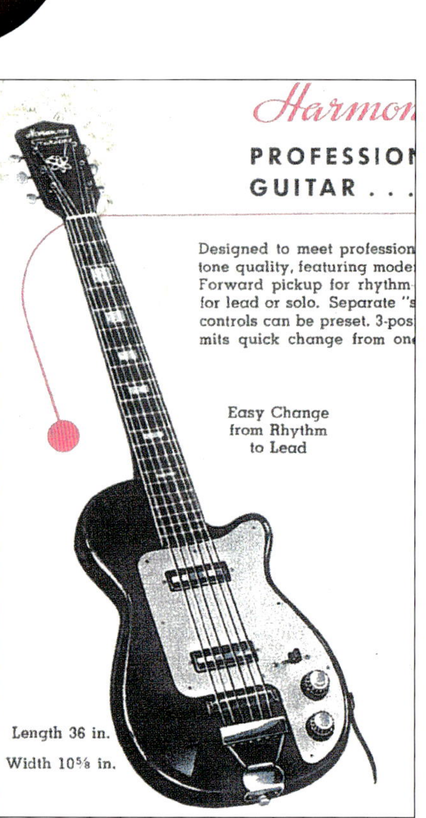

Circa 1955 Harmony H88 "Stratotone Doublet" was designed to meet "professional standards."

DOUBLET"

P ELECTRIC
WAY STYLE.

both. Solid hardwood easy-
Highly polished black lac-
illed ebonized bound finger-
ck position markers. Nickel
heads, compensating tail-
itar strap included.

PORT"

del

ength 36¼ in.
idth 11 in.

Circa 1955 Harmony H42 Newport with the "Harmometal" binding in metallic green. "More colorful – lighter to handle (thinner, too) – that's the story of Harmony's newest – the 'Newport.'"

Circa 1960s Harmony H49 Stratotone was called the Jupiter. This example has a changed bridge.

This guitar was Harmony's first Spanish style solid body guitar. By the early 1960s, Harmony had expanded this line of electric guitars to include a more varied selection of Stratotones. The dot neck Mars came both as a single or double pickup guitar. The more deluxe Stratotone was called the Jupiter. One of my favorites, the Harmony H49, utilized the Harmony blender control that allowed the player to blend between pickups and offered "practically unlimited variations of tone with simplified technique." This guitar was also available as a Silvertone S1423 model. When these Stratotone guitars were sold as Silvertone models, along with other names, most of the time they were similar to their Harmony counterparts except for the logo on the headstock.

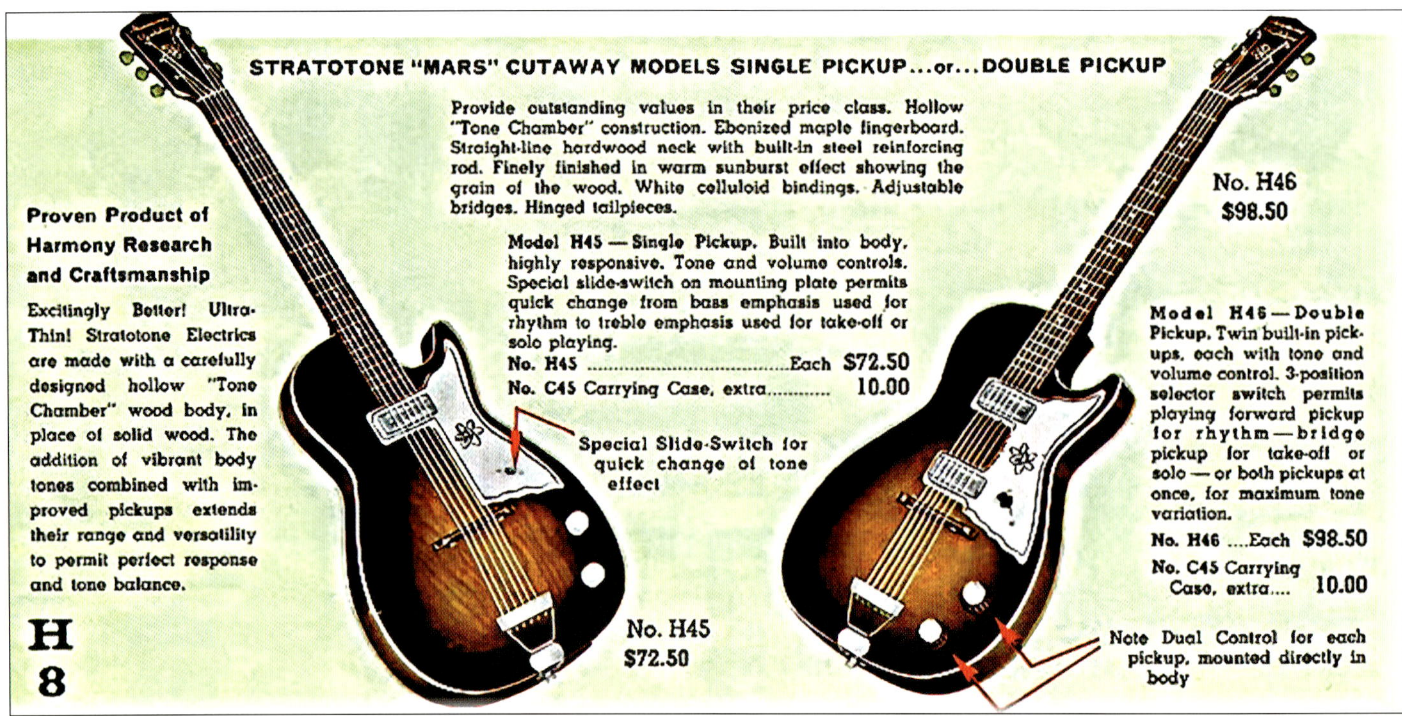

Circa 1958 Harmony H45 Mars, single pickup Stratotone was available under different brands with several pickguard and knob configurations.

The dot neck "Mars" had the new unique feature of a hollow "tone chamber" construction in place of solid wood. *Jay Pilzer photo*

Circa 1960 Silvertone model S1423 that was the sister model to the Harmony H49 Stratotone. It had two DeArmond silver foil pickups along with the "Special effects" blender control.

The Harmony Stratotones disappeared from the Harmony catalog toward the mid-1960s. They were replaced with what was becoming the more traditional solid body electric guitar, the Harmony Silhouette or Bob Kat.

Maybe because these were easier to produce or they were what people wanted at the time, guitar players lost out on a great guitar when Harmony stopped producing the Stratotone.

Circa 1960s Holiday labeled (Harmony made H15) Bob Kat. "The Golden Tone dual pickups designed by DeArmond are angle mounted to provide extended range of tone."

No. H14 No. H15 No. H17

H All SILHOUETTE models have end and shoulder strap pins.

Circa 1960s Harmony H15 or Holiday electric guitar. "Modern design and DeArmond electronics for speed and response, to give you what you want for today's music and playing style!"

Of the different guitars Harmony offered, one style that made its way into the American home was the basic solid body electric. These Harmony electric guitars had everything the aspiring musician needed. Harmony had the ability to manufacture them for the masses and was one of the few American brands that allowed young guitar players the opportunity to start out with an affordable solid body electric.

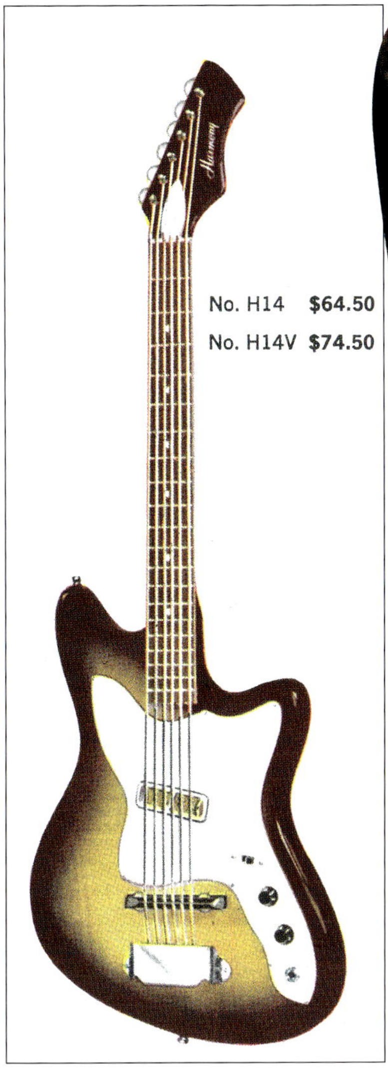

No. H14 **$64.50**

No. H14V **$74.50**

Circa 1968 Harmony H14 Bob Kat electric guitar had a slider switch to vary the sound of the single gold foil pickup. "Short scale for easy chording."

Circa 1971 Harmony H16R "Kolor Kat." Some models have the small body of the H15 Bob Kat (bridge on body), some (later) models have the larger body of the H19 Silhouette (bridge on pickguard).

By 1964, Harmony was offering their Silhouette line of solid body electrics. They still had the Stratotones, but it appeared that producing these solid body guitars was more of the direction Harmony wanted to go. They came out with the H19, the one pickup H14, along with the two pickup H15, and included them in the Harmony solid body catalog through the 1970s.

The Harmony H19 electric guitar, as well as the Bob Kat, had angled pickups for "enhanced tonal effect." The Silvertone version of a Bob Kat guitar had pickups that were *not* angled. The H19 guitar was "A truly professional model," and had block inlays along with a rosewood fingerboard that was bound. These deluxe electric guitar models utilized the new step up DeArmond pickups with adjustable pole pieces.

Circa 1960s Harmony H19 deluxe Silhouette guitar used the "Golden Tone" DeArmond "Mustache-Grill" pickup and was Harmony's finest solid body.

The electric guitars that Harmony made ranged in price and quality, just as their other instruments did. They made many student instruments, with some of the solid body electrics being simple, more fundamental guitars. Their pickups and sound, however, set them apart from the later imports that flooded the market. Models like the Stratotone and the Bob Kat were designed for the beginner player but are still being used professionally today.

They were built for rock and roll and you can bet there was many a garage band that rocked out with a Harmony Bob Kat. They came upon the music scene and caused an impact that affected many young guitar players starting out. As young players outgrew these guitars and went on to bigger and better things, the solid body guitars were almost forgotten. In today's vintage market, if and when you can find a Harmony Bob Kat, you will have a great piece of American rock and roll history.

The Silvertone 1476 and 1478 version of the Bob Kat did not have angled pickups.

CHAPTER 7

HARMONY AMPLIFIERS: MAKING THE MUSIC HEARD

No. H512
$139.50

When the electric guitar was introduced in the late 1940s, Harmony was faced with coming up with amplifiers that would complement their line of Hawaiian electric guitars. The introduction of the Spanish style electric guitar compounded the need for amplifiers to go with their instruments. Harmony amps were made by a variety of manufacturers.

Circa 1960s Harmony H191 guitar amplifier. *Photo courtesy of Rivingtonguitars.com*

1950

MODEL H200-50 SPANISH ELECTRIC C

The guitar is Grand Auditorium size, in rich two-ton
bound and inlaid. Engraved headpiece. Rosewood
tuning keys. Built-in Spanish type "Tone-Emphasi
liking. Has volume and tone control.

5 tube amplifier, excellent tone, high volume. 10 to 1
3 inputs, including microphone. 3 controls for volu
Handsome two-tone cabinet, balanced for easy c
approved.

No.
H2

H2
H5
C5

Circa 1960s Harmony Rally Stripe Amp.

The amps that were offered by Harmony served the purpose of allowing small combos of musicians to replace the big bands and of allowing the music to be heard. They had features that were popular at the time, circuitry and components that were of a similar quality to the other makers, and an appeal that is still sought after today. The older ones, with their 1950s styling, and the small tube amps from the 1960s, all had the look and sound you only get from one of these older amps. Many of them outlived their usefulness and ended up being junked as obsolete and not worth fixing. If you come across a working unit today, it can be a great find for a cool sounding amp.

You plug it in
It turns You on
And you produce sounds you've never heard before. The Harmony prestige sounds you'll love.
Resulting from a lot of experience—78 years of it—a lot of care, a lot of superior engineering. A lot of knowing just how to build fine electric guitars and amplifiers.
So send for your free catalog. You'll view something you've never seen before—pictures and descriptions of 65 different Harmony guitars and amplifiers. Then you can hear them—and select yours—at your favorite music store.
THE Harmony COMPANY
4604 S. KOLIN AVE., CHICAGO, ILL. 60632

CHAPTER 8

ROCKET TO THE STARS AND THE HARMONY PROFESSIONAL GUITARS

Circa 1967 Harmony H54 "Ultra-slim" neck with uniform feel. "'Straight line' narrow fingerboards with celluloid edge binding – short scale for easy chording, 'comping,' or solo work."

As the space age came about in the early 1960s, there were a wide-range of influences on the youth of America. It was the dream of many a kid to shoot for the stars and explore the outer reaches of the universe. Back here on Earth, there was a music revolution going on and it was the dream of many a youth to shoot for rock and roll stardom. The instrument makers at the time were influenced by this parallel dream of the youth of America when naming their instruments.

The Harmony Guitar Company was influenced quite a bit by man's quest to explore the heavens. They had their Meteors; they had their Stratotones; they also had Mars, Mercury, and Jupiter guitars. Harmony named one of its more popular hollow body thin line guitars the Rocket when it was introduced in 1959.

No. H53

No. H54

No. H56

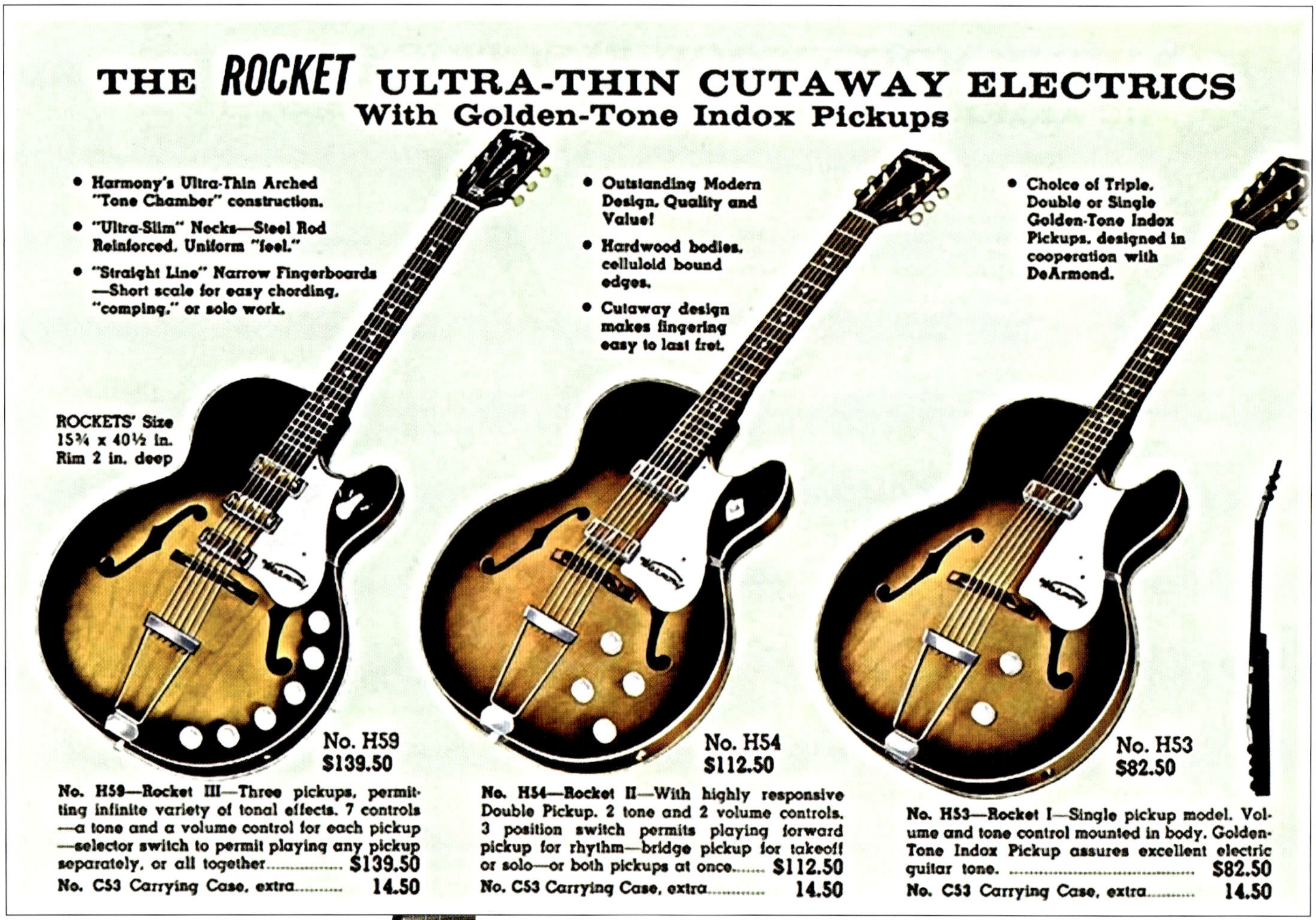

THE ROCKET ULTRA-THIN CUTAWAY ELECTRICS
With Golden-Tone Indox Pickups

- Harmony's Ultra-Thin Arched "Tone Chamber" construction.
- "Ultra-Slim" Necks—Steel Rod Reinforced. Uniform "feel."
- "Straight Line" Narrow Fingerboards—Short scale for easy chording, "comping," or solo work.

- Outstanding Modern Design, Quality and Value!
- Hardwood bodies, celluloid bound edges.
- Cutaway design makes fingering easy to last fret.

- Choice of Triple, Double or Single Golden-Tone Indox Pickups, designed in cooperation with DeArmond.

ROCKETS' Size 15¾ x 40½ in. Rim 2 in. deep

No. H59
$139.50

No. H59—Rocket III—Three pickups, permitting infinite variety of tonal effects. 7 controls—a tone and a volume control for each pickup—selector switch to permit playing any pickup separately, or all together.......... **$139.50**
No. C53 Carrying Case, extra.......... **14.50**

No. H54
$112.50

No. H54—Rocket II—With highly responsive Double Pickup. 2 tone and 2 volume controls. 3 position switch permits playing forward pickup for rhythm—bridge pickup for takeoff or solo—or both pickups at once....... **$112.50**
No. C53 Carrying Case, extra.......... **14.50**

No. H53
$82.50

No. H53—Rocket I—Single pickup model. Volume and tone control mounted in body. Golden-Tone Indox Pickup assures excellent electric guitar tone. **$82.50**
No. C53 Carrying Case, extra.......... **14.50**

Circa 1962 Harmony sunburst H54 two pickup Rocket. "Outstanding modern design, quality and value!"

Circa 1960 Harmony H59 Rocket in sunburst which used the DeArmond foil face pickups. "Harmony's ultra-thin arched 'tone chamber' construction."

From the Rocket's introduction in 1959 through the early 1970s, when Harmony gave up guitar production, these guitars changed only a little and would utilize the guitar technology that was available. The Harmony Rocket came into existence to satisfy the need for a thin, hollow body guitar. They would evolve from the early 1960s sunburst single cutaways to the red versions of the Rocket that are more commonly seen. Whether it was one of these Rockets, or an upgrade to their top of the line H75 guitar, this style of guitar is still quite desirable. As a cheaper alternative to the thin Gibson hollow body guitars, these guitars gained in popularity as the music revolution took off.

Harmony H59 three pickup Rocket with the earlier DeArmond gold foil pickups. Later these were replaced with the adjustable pole DeArmond pickup.

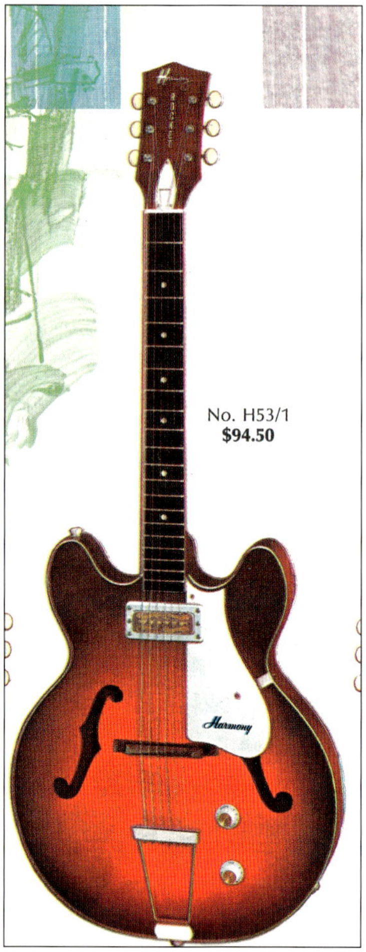

No. H53/1
$94.50

Harmony Rockets became double cutaway guitars by the 1970s.

Circa 1968 Harmony H78 "top-of-the-line" three-pickup electric guitar with Bigsby tailpiece along with its Silvertone version of the model 1454, single cutaway guitar.

Circa 1967 Harmony red Rocket started using the "Golden-Tone" pickup with adjustable poles and came in the same one-, two-, or three-pickup models as the earlier guitars.

Harmony Guitars, although they catered to the beginner, also tried to market guitars to professional players. These guitars were a higher quality instrument: "Jewel like beauty . . . superb styling . . . in these fine precision-made, professional cutaway electrics." This line of guitars incorporated a variety of features that brought them up a notch from the quality and price point of other Harmony guitars.

Circa 1967 Harmony by Heath version of an H78 with Bigsby. *Photo courtesy of David Fuhrman*

Heathkit, the electronics kit company, offered a model that was the same as the Harmony H78 electric guitar, "With Bigsby true vibrato tailpiece and three pickups . . . DeArmond designed for today's sound." It did get a designation that it was a TG-46 Heathkit model number. *Photo courtesy of David Fuhrman*

Circa 1968 Harmony H77 "top-of-the-line" three-pickup electric guitar. "Double Cutaway" – sixteen frets clear of body – the highest registers easily fingered."

Another one of my favorite guitars that was introduced around 1960 was the H75 double cutaway, triple pickup electric guitar. This family of guitars had three tone and volume knobs and three on/off toggle controls to give the guitar a variety of sounds, with all the "bells, knobs and whistles" one could possibly want. The DeArmond designed pickups with adjustable magnetic pole pieces, along with the nine controls, gave an "infinite choice of tonal effects." The headstock of this top-of-the-line Harmony guitar was overlaid with a tortoise, engraved veneer that matched the tortoise pickguard and trim. As with some of the earlier better grade guitars, this headstock veneer set them apart from the less expensive guitars.

No. H75
$275.00

No. H77
$275.00

Circa 1957 Harmony H65 electric Spanish guitar with cutaway, in a blonde finish. "Harmony's new functional design to help your playing . . . thin model body, 2¾ in. deep, makes playing more comfortable . . . short scale, 24¼ in., for easier rhythm or take off, less fatigue."

Circa 1957 Harmony H65 electric Spanish guitar with cutaway also came in a sunburst finish.

With the use of a variety of DeArmond pickups, Harmony was able to achieve a sound and tone that is still desirable. Advertisements for the H75 and H77 guitars claimed, "Three pickups DeArmond designed for today's sound."

A variety of DeArmond pickups were used on most of the electrics made by Harmony. One exception was the H62 model that was a set neck, full body depth electric guitar that used a Gibson P-13 pickup. This guitar, with its own unique voicing, was not a bad choice for the budget minded jazz guitarist and today can be seen being used by many rockabilly guitarists.

Circa 1960 Silvertone H63 Espanada that was the black version of their professional jazz guitar. Earlier ones were the metal bound Espanada guitars. Later they had the traditional plastic binding and were a little narrower in depth. *Photo courtesy of Bananaguitars.com*

By 1973, the finer instruments were no longer listed as "Professional" guitars and they were the last of the deluxe guitars made by Harmony. There were no Meteors being produced by Harmony, only Rockets and Rebels.

Harmony's earlier "Professional" guitars from the 1960s had achieved a level of respect; it was hard to regain that respect in the 1970s as their fall from grace took place.

Circa 1960 Harmony H62 Electric Archtop jazz guitar was listed in the catalog as blonde, but some sunburst guitars have been found.

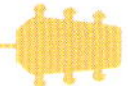

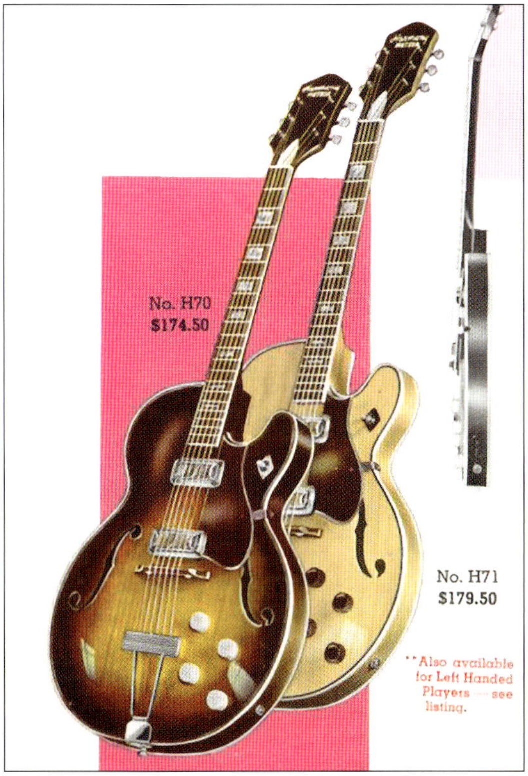
No. H70
$174.50
No. H71
$179.50
**Also available for Left Handed Players — see listing.

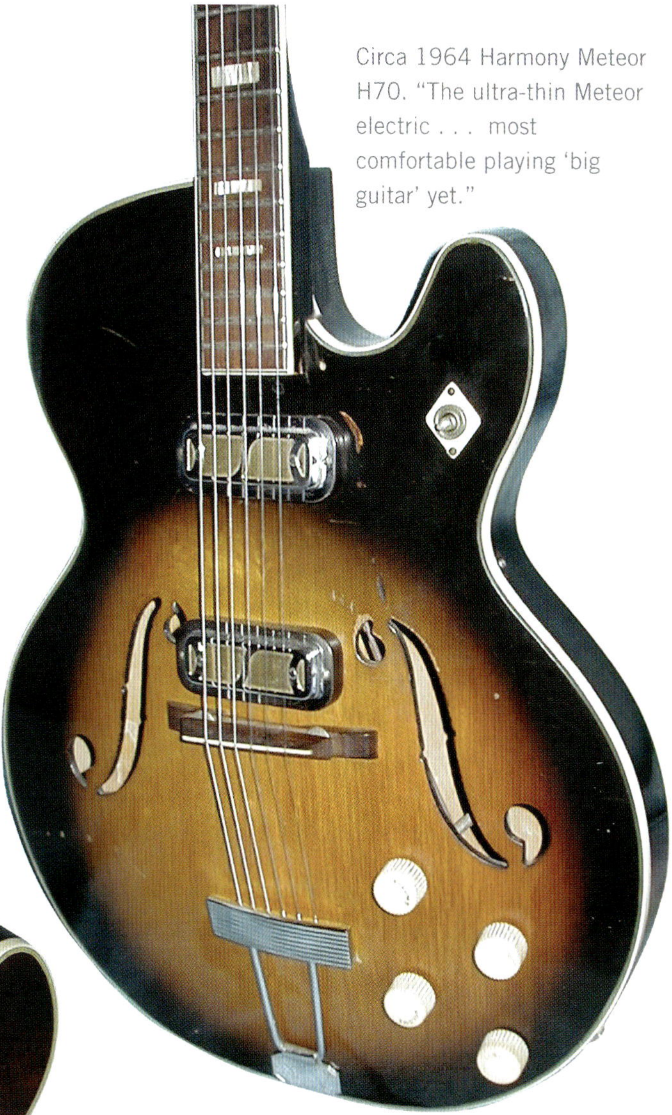

Circa 1964 Harmony Meteor H70. "The ultra-thin Meteor electric . . . most comfortable playing 'big guitar' yet."

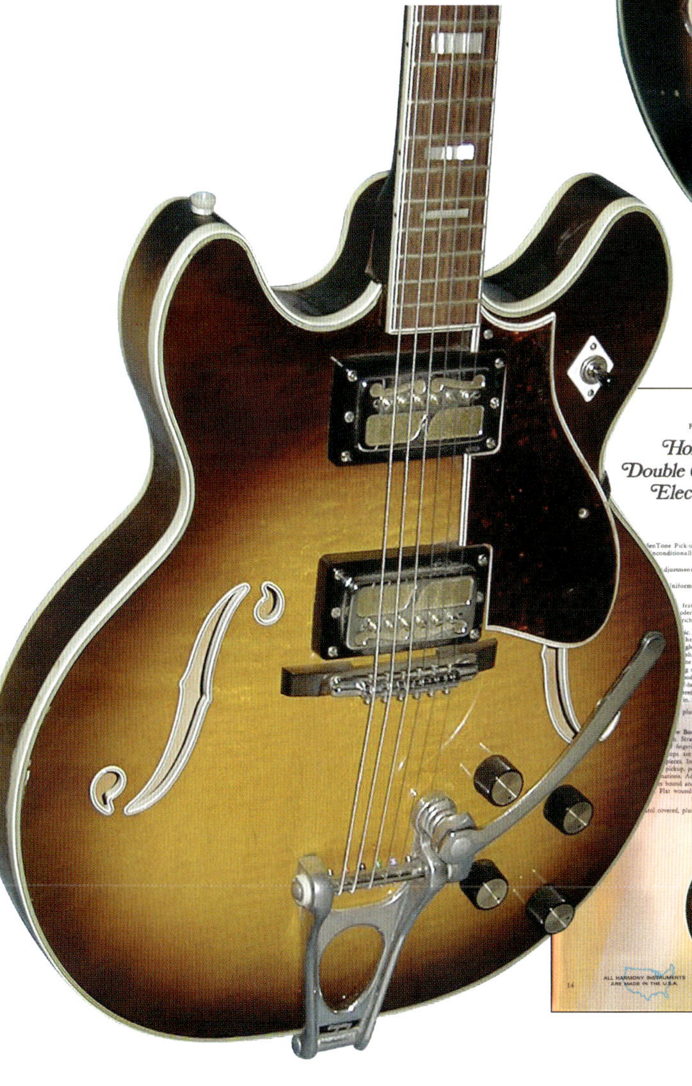

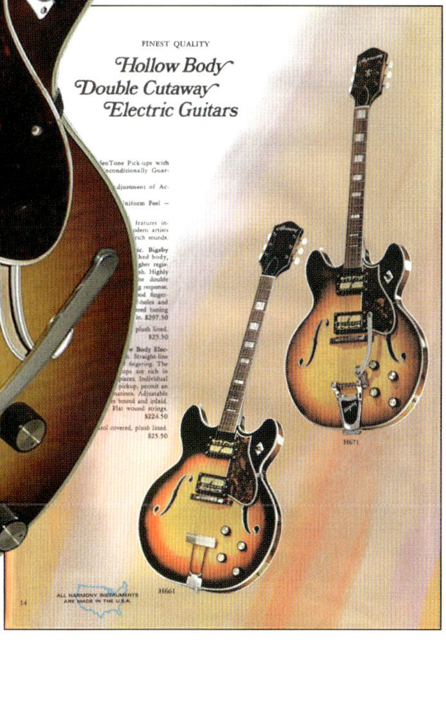
FINEST QUALITY
Hollow Body
Double Cutaway
Electric Guitars
H671
H661
ALL HARMONY INSTRUMENTS ARE MADE IN THE U.S.A.
34

Circa 1972 Harmony H671 was a deviation from the three pickup electric guitars. This "Professional series" guitar had two of the larger DeArmond pickups and a tremolo tailpiece. The "f" holes were bound on this model.

Circa 1970s Harmony H68 Jazz guitar had bound "f" holes and larger DeArmond pickups. It appeared as though Harmony just added pickups and electronics to the H1310 acoustic model.

Harmony's line of professional grade instruments did survive the 1960s but there were few other Harmony electric guitars from the line that survived like the Rockets did. The Harmony Rocket found today, as when it was made, is an affordable American vintage guitar. It brought together features and an appeal that continues to capture the dreams of the baby boomer generation while also appealing to Generation X.

Circa 1970 Harmony H72 electric guitar. "Striking modern design f-holes. This guitar also had straight line tuning keys."

CHAPTER 9

REBEL WITH A CAUSE

Circa 1971 Harmony H82 "Rebel" double pickup electric guitar. "Great for playing in a group, or for your own entertainment."

The 1960s got into full swing by the end of the decade. There was a war going on and revolution was in the air. Rock and roll was alive. Kids were getting electric guitars so they could make their statements and be heard. There was no better name for the new, innovative guitar Harmony was developing than the Harmony "Rebel" guitar.

Stick-Shift* Controls
on Harmony's New
Hollow Body
"REBEL" Electrics
are Revolutionary!

A "Spectacular" in tone and volume controls—now you just move your "stick-shift"* on straight line for a new ease and accuracy in producing your favorite effects. You'll know your settings — visually. See a new REBEL—try it—you'll believe it.

No. H82
$109.50

No. H82G
$109.50

No. H81
$90.00

Amazingly Low in Price for Harmony's Standard of Quality

Model H82. Harmony "Rebel" Double Pickup Electric Guitar. Great for playing in a group, or for your own entertainment. Note the double cutaway design of the body. It is thin, too—only 1¾ in. deep and light in weight. Its hollow tone chamber construction assures a pleasing acoustic resonance to balance the "electronic" tone.

Built of laminated maple, with celluloid bindings on top and back edges. Hardwood neck is reinforced with an adjustable Torque-Lok rod. The ovalled ebonized maple fingerboard has 7 inlaid position markers.

The electronics were designed in cooperation with DeArmond. 6 controls—Rebel's "stick-shift"* volume and tone controls are the newest development in the guitar field.

You can long be proud of your "Rebel's" finish. It is a blend of brown and red shaded tones, against a deep yellow highlite, all beautifully polished.

No. H82. Size 14 x 38 x 1¾ in. With double pickups **$109.50**

Model H82G. Same as Model H82 Electric Guitar, but in the popular Avocado shading, beautifully polished. With double pickups. **$109.50**

Model H81. Same in color and quality as Model H82 above, but with single pickup, quick tone change slide switch, one volume and one tone slide control. **$90.00**

No. HC81—Carrying Case for above models **$15.00**

*STICK-SHIFT—a Harmony exclusive.

9

Circa 1971 Harmony H81 single pickup Rebel guitar.

Circa 1971 Harmony H82 Rebel utilized a series of slide controls for tone and volume settings.

The Rebel was one of the more unusual hollow body Harmony electrics to be designed by them. They all had a type "W" vibrato tailpiece and most distinctive, double Florentine (pointed) cutaways. The Harmony Rebel allowed for the adjustment of volume and tone with a series of slide switches: "Easy, visual, stick-shift controls." The catalog showed how you could produce your favorite effects by knowing your settings with a visual reference.

As Harmony approached its final years, the quality of their new guitars stood out. These new models were developed with innovative designs and features, and incorporated the latest technology. The components that Harmony became known for were kept in place. They would add contemporary ideas, since they were striving to compete with the big boys. Harmony was trying to make instruments that would appeal to the professional player. Even though their guitars got better, it was increasingly difficult to produce an instrument that could compete with imports, which were beginning to flood the market. Although they weren't able to compete, Harmony kept trying into the 1970s and right up until their final days, making a gallant effort. They were a Rebel with a cause . . . to survive.

Circa 1970s Silvertone version of a Harmony Rebel except it did not have the slider controls and did not use the adjustable pole DeArmond pickups.

CHAPTER 10

HARMONY BASS GUITARS: HOLDING DOWN THE BOTTOM!

Circa 1964 Harmony H22 hollow body electric bass guitar. Auditorium size "Ultra-Thin hollow Tone Chamber" with its laminated maple body.

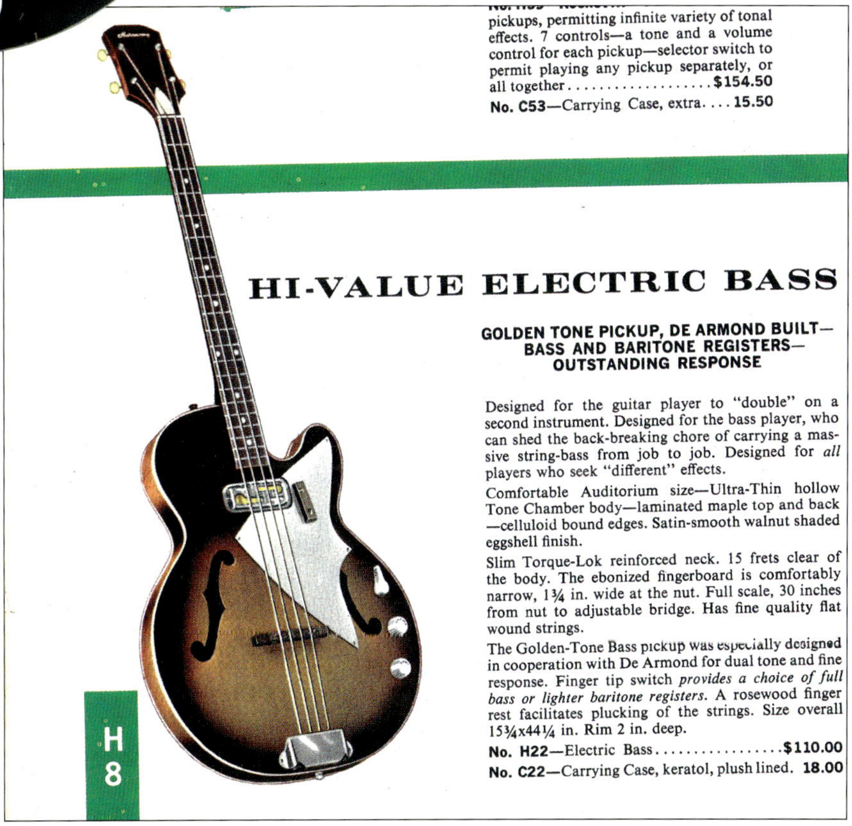

pickups, permitting infinite variety of tonal effects. 7 controls—a tone and a volume control for each pickup—selector switch to permit playing any pickup separately, or all together.................. **$154.50**

No. C53—Carrying Case, extra.... **15.50**

HI-VALUE ELECTRIC BASS

GOLDEN TONE PICKUP, DE ARMOND BUILT—BASS AND BARITONE REGISTERS—OUTSTANDING RESPONSE

Designed for the guitar player to "double" on a second instrument. Designed for the bass player, who can shed the back-breaking chore of carrying a massive string-bass from job to job. Designed for *all* players who seek "different" effects.

Comfortable Auditorium size—Ultra-Thin hollow Tone Chamber body—laminated maple top and back—celluloid bound edges. Satin-smooth walnut shaded eggshell finish.

Slim Torque-Lok reinforced neck. 15 frets clear of the body. The ebonized fingerboard is comfortably narrow, 1¾ in. wide at the nut. Full scale, 30 inches from nut to adjustable bridge. Has fine quality flat wound strings.

The Golden-Tone Bass pickup was especially designed in cooperation with De Armond for dual tone and fine response. Finger tip switch *provides a choice of full bass or lighter baritone registers.* A rosewood finger rest facilitates plucking of the strings. Size overall 15¾x44¼ in. Rim 2 in. deep.

No. H22—Electric Bass................ **$110.00**

No. C22—Carrying Case, keratol, plush lined. **18.00**

H 8

Circa 1960s Harmony H22 had a "batwing" pickguard and offered a unique look to the Harmony catalog.

As the electric bass grew in popularity during the mid 1950s, Harmony was working to develop an instrument to meet the demand and jumped into the market. The 1961 Harmony catalog listed the H22 as the "Hi-Value" electric bass and marketed it "For the bass player that would like to shed the back breaking chore of carrying a massive string-bass from job to job." During the 1960s, there was a growing need for a greater selection of bass guitars. With this need in mind, Harmony expanded their line to include the H27, a double pickup, double cutaway bass, along with the H25 solid body Silhouette bass featuring an electric solid body design similar to their six-string Silhouette. The H27 model was designed to meet the standards of the professional player and was in keeping with the top of the line Harmony instruments that offered a tortoise headstock overlay.

Circa 1960s Harmony H25 solid body Silhouette bass.

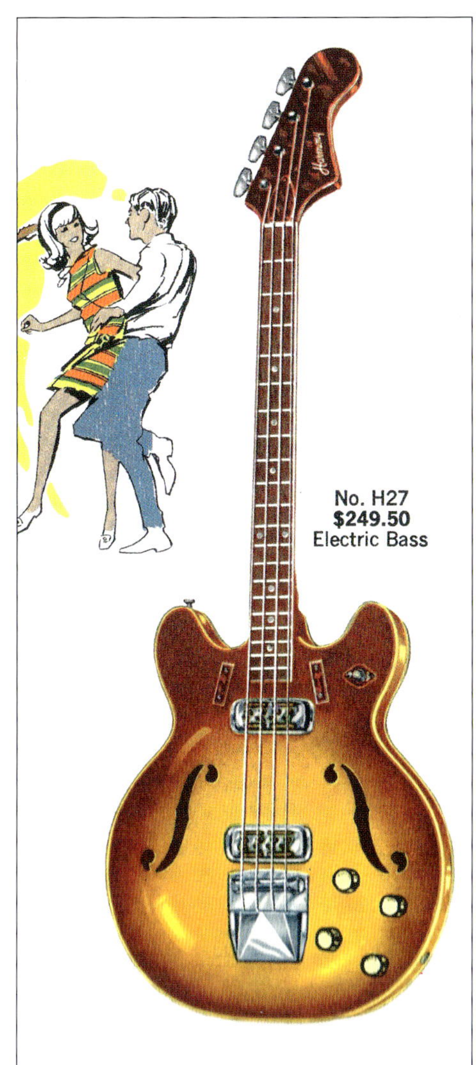

Harmony H420 bass was a 70s version of the sunburst H27 found in the 1960s.
Photo courtesy of www.nortonguitarworks.com

The Harmony bass has become one of the more desirable "off brand" vintage bass guitars. The Harmony H22 bass had been one of the more requested instruments since I started dealing in vintage Harmony guitars. With its single cutaway and DeArmond pickup, the H22 has a look and sound that fits many genres of music.

I have been using the H22 for some blues gigs; the rich, warm sound from the instrument is superior to the sound of my other basses. Its rich low end is something that many bass players search for.

Harmony bass guitars had a certain appeal to the beginner players. Some of them emulated the Fender style, but Harmony also made hollow bodied bass guitars. These guitars, like others, were generally not of the same quality as those they tried to copy, but players were able to afford them and get an instrument they could utilize.

Chapter 11

HARMONY CARIBBEAN AND COLORAMA GUITARS, AND THE DIFFERENT, UNUSUAL, OR NOT SO POPULAR GUITARS

Circa 1955 Harmony No.1003 copper and Sahara yellow Caribbean guitar, another variation of the "Holiday Colorama" series.

The year was 1955, and Harmony came out with a new bright and shiny original look. Harmony instruments took on a new concept of color and design for guitars. The bright flower power colors of the 1960s and the Deco look of the 1930s merged together to give these Harmony guitars a unique look. Ahead of their time or thirty years too late, this unique look set them apart from other guitars during this period.

Circa 1955 Harmony Caribbean No.1002 acoustic flat top, reef coral/white was just one choice of the six "Holiday Colorama" color combinations.

The Harmony Caribbean guitars, with their delicate pastel and metallic finishes, were inspired by the colors found in the fabulous vacation spots of the tropical seas to the south. Some of these guitars were also set off with metal trim. This made for an unusual looking guitar with lines that had a Deco look.

The Harmony flat top guitar line had six different guitars that had Holiday Colorama color combinations and were as distinct looking as any guitar I've seen. The Harmony Colorama style of their Stella Sundale guitars also brought this surge of vibrant color to Harmony's lowest priced flat tops. The graphic design and color seemed to be on the cutting edge of what they coined "A modern trend—the swing into the new concept of mass color."

Circa 1955 Harmony No.902 Pacific blue and white Stella Sundale guitar. "Sundale brings a surge of vibrant color in Harmony's lowest price range."

Circa 1955 Harmony No.1221 Pacific blue and dawn blue Colorama Catalina archtop guitar. "Modern two-tone contrast gives accent to the graceful arched tops and backs of these Catalina models."

Circa 1955 Harmony No.1220 Catalina guitar charcoal grey and pink color.

Harmony Holiday Colorama

CATALINA Arched Guitars

Color . . . color in modern two-tone contrast . . . gives accent to the graceful arched tops and backs of these Catalina models.

Guitars are Auditorium size, 40½ x 15¾ in., of dependable hardwood construction. Fitted with gear-type machine heads, bone nuts, celluloid guard-plates mounted on bracket, adjustable bridges, nickel plated tailpieces. Elevated type fingerboards, accurately fretted. Carefully finished in lacquer enamels with striped edges.

No. 1221—Catalina Guitar, Pacific Blue and Dawn Blue........ $28.50

No. 1220—Catalina Guitar, Charcoal Grey and Pink....... $28.50

The Colorama guitars at this time seemed to be the main core of Harmony's guitar line. Ahead of their time, these Harmony guitars are some of the more interesting American-made instruments I've owned, to date. Their bold color and unique binding, along with their other innovative manufacturing ideas, made for some real gems from this period.

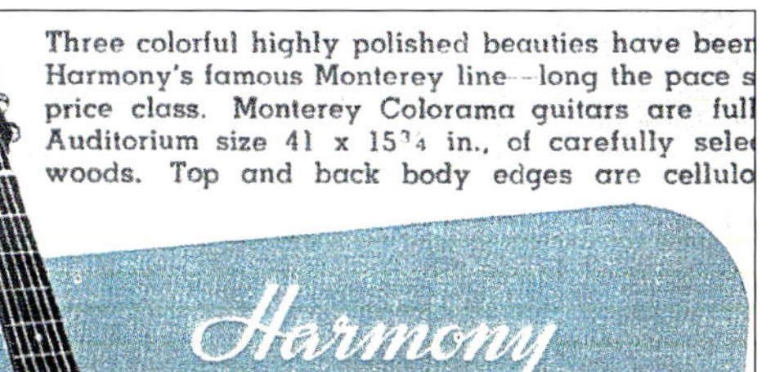

Three colorful highly polished beauties have been
Harmony's famous Monterey line—long the pace s
price class. Monterey Colorama guitars are full
Auditorium size 41 x 15¾ in., of carefully sele
woods. Top and back body edges are cellulo

Harmony
MONTCLAIR
GUITARS

In Auditorium and Grand Auditorium Sizes

At the forefront of modern guitar styling. The aerojet-like application of bright Harmometal gives brilliant contrast to the highly polished, rich-black finish. Harmometal top and back edges add beauty and protection.

Fine craftmanship . . . ovalled fingerboard, with celluloid bound edges . . . compensating tailpiece . . . thick plastic pickguard.

No. 956—Auditorium size, 40½ x 15¾ in. **$45.00**

No. 956S—Grand Auditorium size, 40½ x 16⅝ in. **$49.50**

Circa 1955 Harmony No.956 Montclair. "The aero-jet like application of bright Harmometal gives brilliant contrast to the highly polished, rich-black finish." This example is missing the white pickguard.

Circa 1955 Harmony No.956 Montclair and Espanada guitars utilized the Harmometal binding not only to protect the edges but to add a contrasting graphic design to the rich-black top.

There was not much that compared in uniqueness to some of Harmony's archtops from this period. Some of the more distinctive looking guitars were the Harmony Espanada and Montclair No.956, with their metal binding. These guitars were both metal bound and trimmed with Harmony's Harmometal. This binding was designed to protect the edges on the guitar, but was more reminiscent of the edge found on the Formica countertops and kitchen tables of the 1950s. "An extraordinary instrument for the advanced player," as the catalog stated. While the Montclair name referred to several different models, they often were a non-cutaway archtop guitar.

Circa 1967 Harmony H66 Vibrajet electric guitar. This guitar offered a built-in tremolo circuit, at your fingertips. "Built into this handsome neo-cutaway double pickup electric is a skillfully engineered transistorized and miniaturized assembly (made in America)."

Harmony always had interesting instruments that were different or on the cutting edge of guitar technology along with common instruments that were never as popular. They were inventive and creative with the colors of the Harmony Caribbean guitars and always strived to come out with some new and interesting features; their inventory included guitars that were a little different or had lower production than the mainstream instruments other manufacturers were making.

Some of these instruments were common, like classical guitars, and some were new models that were never as popular as the guitars that were seen more often. All were offered by Harmony in some capacity during its history. Given the lower production and the time that has passed, some of these guitars are less available today; some you might rarely see.

HARMONY FLAT TOP "CUTAWAY" GUITAR
Grand Auditorium Size 16¼" wide

1200

The new H40 Uno-tone guitar was an acoustic guitar with a built in pickup that could be played through an amplifier, "with no tone-loss or tone-change." This Auditorium size acoustic flat top had a concealed "Tone-Emphasizer" P-13 pickup built in the end of the fingerboard. *Photo courtesy of Joe Stone*

There has never been a lot of interest to explore the diversity of the classical line in any great depth, but to quote Willie Moseley in his book *Classic Guitars, USA*: "Cir? Who knows, Who cares?" Nice instruments, but little interest.

Circa 1970s Harmony H79 electric twelve-string guitar, Harmony's finest twelve-string electric guitar.
Photo courtesy of Joe Stone

Circa 1960s Harmony Stella twelve-string guitar. *Photo courtesy of vintagebluesguitars.com*

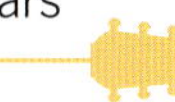

Harmony
HAWAIIAN
ELECTRIC
GUITARS

H-5

Distinguished, modern styled guitar, inlaid. Rich mahogany sunburst polished finish. 23" scale. Plastic fingerboard and handrest. Individual tuning keys. "Tone Emphasizer" pickup, volume and tone controls.

H5	Guitar only	$ 59.50-A
C5	Carrying Case, extra	8.50-A
H5-205	Guitar with 5 tube Amp.	157.00-A
H5-191	Guitar with 3 tube Amp.	117.00-A

H-3

Here is the superb "Tone-Emphasizer" pickup in a moderately priced guitar. The hardwood body is attractively finished in lustrous brown lacquer-enamel with gold contrast-stripes. Has handrest.

H3	Guitar only	$ 52.00-A
C3	Carrying Case, extra	8.50-A
H3-205	Guitar with 5-tube Amp.	149.50-A
H3-191	Guitar with 3-tube Amp.	109.50-A

H-1

A practical guitar for student or class use. Pebbled leather-effect lacquer finish. 27-fret ivory-stenciled fingerboard. Dependable "Tone-Emphasizer" pickup, tone and volume controls.

H1	Guitar only	$ 45.00-A
C1	Carrying Case	8.50-A
H1-191	Guitar with 3-tube Amp.	102.50-A
H1-205	Guitar with 5-tube Amp.	142.50-A

2

Early Harmony H1 lap steel guitar. The model number was reused for later lap steels.

Harmony offered a variety of lap steel guitars throughout the years. These electric guitars existed through the 1950s, and were consistent with the original lap steels made in earlier years. The H5, H3, and H1 of the early 1950s gave way to the H7 Roy Smeck signature instrument by 1962, which was offered along with the popular H1 model steel guitar.

Although lap steel guitars outlived their demand with the coming of the Spanish electric guitar, they remained in the Harmony catalog through the 1970s. A necessity in Hawaiian music and some country and western, lap steel guitars just weren't being used that much in modern rock and roll.

Unique, different, not so popular, or the most popular style of the times, Harmony always had a lot to offer. Considering the diverse models they made, they always had a quality and price point that appealed to a broad range of guitar players.

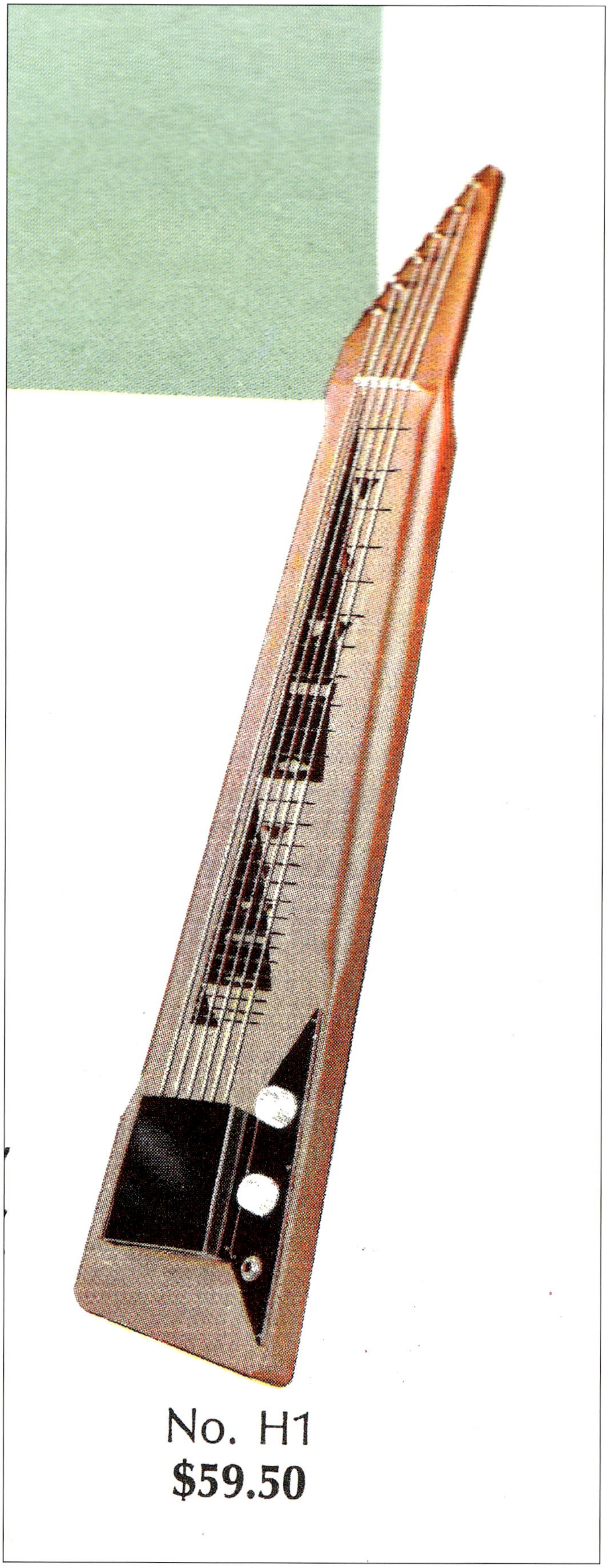

No. H1
$59.50

Circa 1962 Harmony H1 lap steel with copper bronze lacquer. Later model H601 had a different tailpiece and no pickup cover.

CHAPTER 12

ROY SMECK: "WIZARD OF THE STRINGS"

Circa 1962 Roy Smeck 7208, distributed by Montgomery Ward.

Roy Smeck was one of the few professional fretted instrument performers to achieve fame on the world stage and became one of the artists who had Harmony signature models. Coming out of the vaudeville era and making his way onto the silver screen, he became known as "The Wizard of the Strings." He became known for his promotion of happy music and continued performing until his death, at age ninety-four, in 1994.

Circa 1960s Harmony Roy Smeck No.555 ukulele.

Roy Smeck

No. H555
$15.00

The early flat tops and archtops started showing up with the Roy Smeck name in the early 1940s, after his association with Gibson ended. Over the years, there was an assortment of Roy Smeck endorsed guitars. The H56 Electric Spanish archtop, that Harmony came out with in the mid-1950s was designed by Smeck and was one of Harmony's professional models at this time.

Roy Smeck, known for his ukulele playing, endorsed one of the more popular ukuleles, the Roy Smeck No.555. Harmony's banjo line included both the Roy Smeck five string and tenor banjo, both with a plastic reso-tone rim and resonator, and were both referred to as a "professional banjo with ringing tone."

By the mid-1970s, the Smeck guitars had disappeared from the catalog. While the ukes, Hawaiian guitars, and banjos survived, Roy Smeck had lost his appeal to the baby boomer guitarist. The age of vaudeville had waned, as had the popularity of this fretted instrument virtuoso. At the same time the Harmony Guitar Company was struggling to survive, with or without its number one endorsee.

Circa 1962 Roy Smeck 7208, similar in design to a H49 Stratotone, with its geometric pickguard design.

Roy Smeck

MODEL

A striking concept in Hawaiian guitar design, developed for Roy Smeck's professional appearances. Incorporates highly responsive pickup, special tone control, and volume control with extended handle for special effects. Two-level body, devised for ease of holding in playing position. Sweeping curves are given sharp contrast and eye appeal by the gleaming polished black and white finish. Plastic fingerboard and handrest. Nickel plated machine heads. Extension cord.

No. H7 Guitar only—Size 31¾ x 8 in......... **$99.50**

No. C7 Carrying Case, hard shell, extra **27.50**

The Roy Smeck H7 Electric Hawaiian guitar, developed for his professional appearances, and available with three legs as an added option to make it into a "Console" guitar.

CHAPTER 13

HARMONY'S FOLK INSTRUMENTS

Harmony Baritone Ukulele. Made of seasoned mahogar
nicely figured, well finished. Fingerboard of Brazilian ro
wood. Inlaid position markers. Tuning keys are fine quali
strings are carefully gauged nylon. Length of scale 19½
width of body 10"; length 13⅞"; length overall 29¾".
No. 695 .... Each $39.

Ukuleles
by HARMONY

"Accurately Molded"
Easy-to-Play FINGERBOAR

Harmony's creativeness a
craftsmen produced this
genious "Accurately Molde
polystyrene plastic fing
board for moderately pric
wood ukuleles. Offers fretti
that is perfection itself. Us
on standard size models. N
available on Concert a
Tenor sizes.

No. 125½
$8.95

No. 83
$8.95

No. 119½
$9.50

No. 98
$10.75

Excellent beginner's ukulele. Stand-

The Vita guitars were unique looking with their pear shape, "seal" sound holes, and airplane bridge. This is an example of the H1550 tenor guitar.

Harmony, mostly known for their guitars, supplied music lovers with an assortment of other instruments they could afford and enjoy. Their banjos, ukuleles, and mandolins provided the opportunity for people to try different folk instruments. By looking through Harmony's catalogs, you can see the large variety of instruments they were offering at price points that were consistent with their guitars.

Circa 1960s Harmony baritone uke.

Not since the early part of the twentieth century and the time of the 1915 San Francisco Exposition, when there was a Hawaiian music craze taking place, has the ukulele been as popular as now. During that period, Harmony was the largest manufacturer of ukuleles in America. Through the 1950s, Harmony continued to be a leading manufacturer of ukuleles. They had endorsees like Johnny Marvin and Roy Smeck who had models named for them, along with an assortment of beginner to better quality ukes.

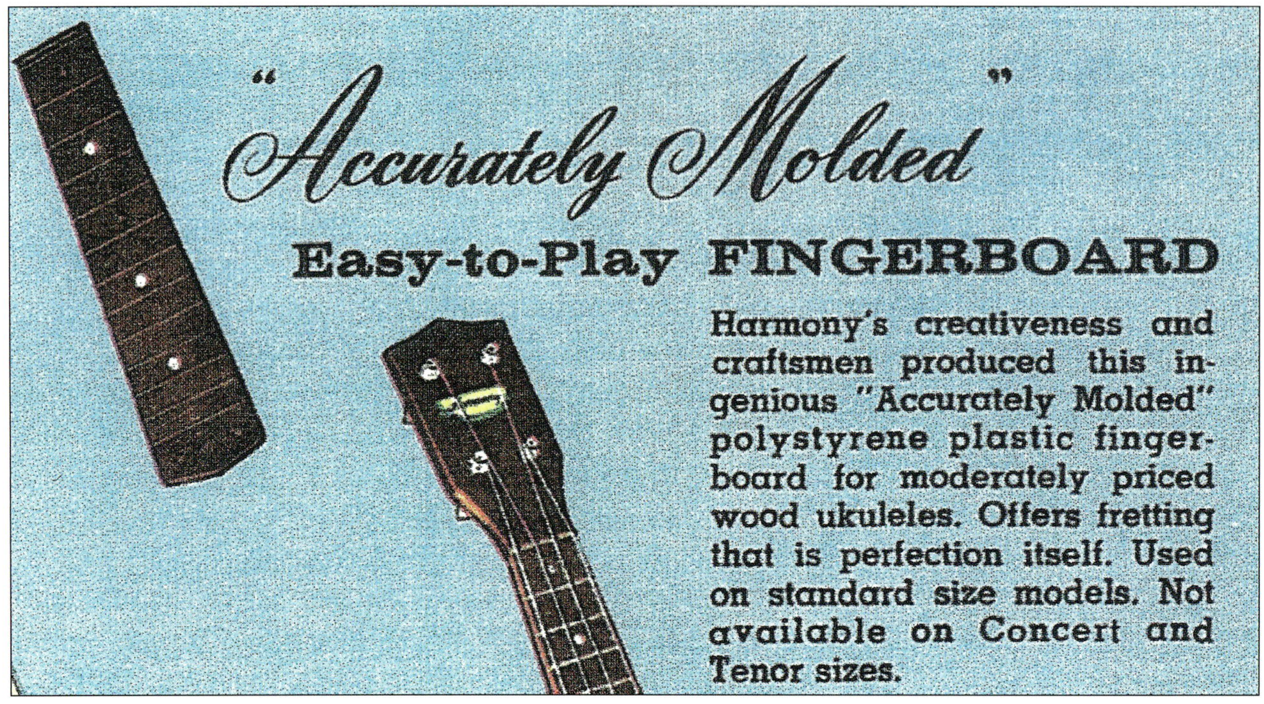

Harmony would start using a plastic fingerboard that was "Accurately Molded" on their soprano ukuleles.

The Harmony Roy Smeck No.8125 tenor banjo survived in the Harmony catalog through the 1960s and was offered as one of their professional banjos.

Harmony was in the forefront of ukulele making. They had a wide selection of ukes, and stated in their catalog: "For fun or educational purpose . . . (that) gave tangible evidence of their leadership."

By today's standards of manufacturing, they did not compare with the quality of the reasonably priced ukuleles that are now being produced, but they did and still find their way into many players' hands.

Harmony's banjos reflected a similar price point and variety as their guitars. Their banjo line included the Roy Smeck models, "As a Professional Banjo with powerful ringing tone." In addition to these better banjos, Harmony also had a standard sixteen bracket banjo that was available as a tenor or five string banjo. Catering to the aspiring student, these less expensive banjos gave beginners an affordable option. The "Glamour of the traditional Folk banjo" was made affordable to the avid banjo student with these mass-produced Harmony instruments.

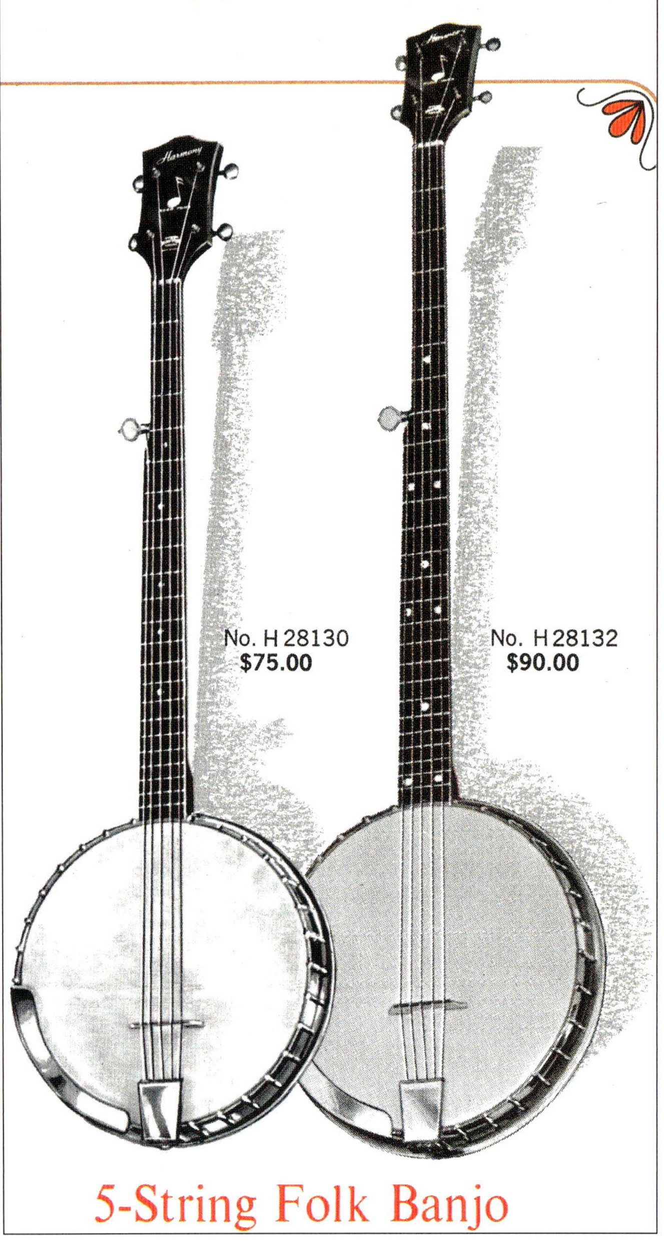

Harmony's folk instruments reflected a similar price point and variety as their guitars and ran parallel to other instruments in their catalog.

Harmony MANDOLINS

417

410

331

Monterey Arched spruce top Mandolin. Richly shaded mahogany color polished finish. Celluloid edge bindings. Suspended rosewood fingerboard, with binding. Bone nut. Adjustable rosewood bridge. Plated tailpiece. Fine tone quality, easy fingering.
No. 417 ....Each $40.00

Monterey Arched Model Mandolin, made of seasoned birch, with celluloid top edge. Hardwood neck; ebonized fingerboard, accurately fretted. Celluloid pickguard. Adjustable bridge. Plated tailpiece. Mahogany shaded eggshell lacquer finish.
No. 410 ....Each $27.50

Stella moderately priced lute-style mandolin of birch construction, pleasingly shaded in reddish mahogany and grained. White striping on top edge and soundhole. Hard maple fingerboard, accurately fretted. White celluloid pickguard.
No. 331 ....Each $20.00

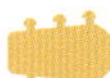

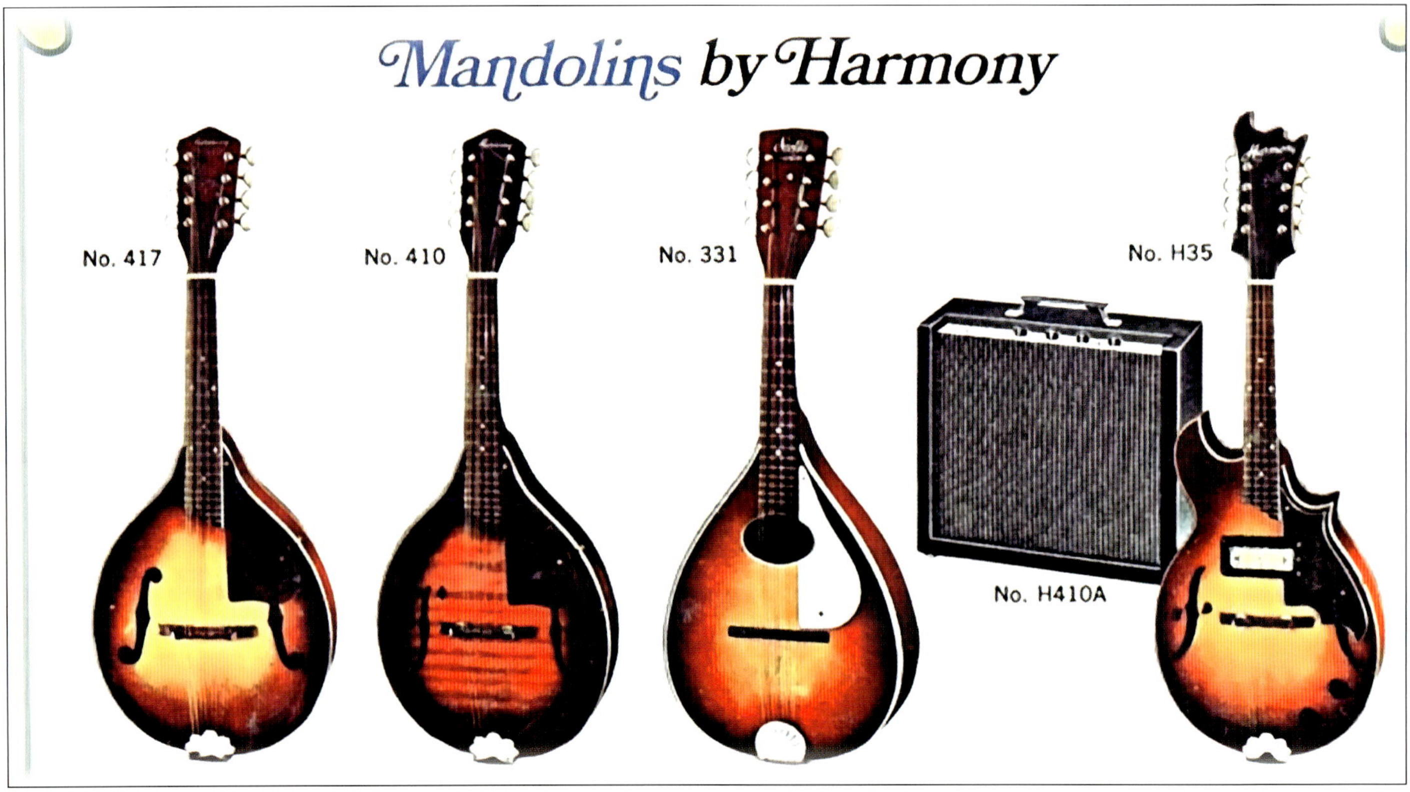
Mandolins by Harmony
No. 417
No. 410
No. 331
No. H35
No. H410A

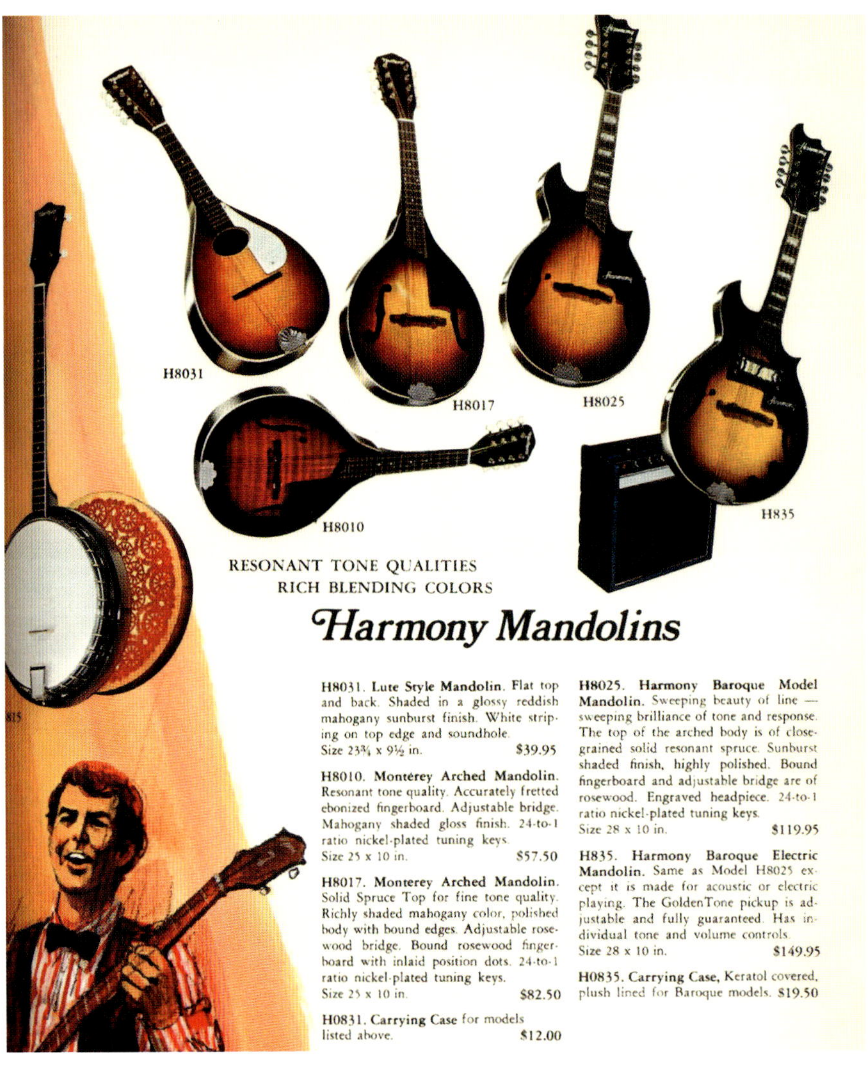

H8031
H8017
H8025
H8010
H835
RESONANT TONE QUALITIES
RICH BLENDING COLORS
Harmony Mandolins
H8031. Lute Style Mandolin. Flat top and back. Shaded in a glossy reddish mahogany sunburst finish. White striping on top edge and soundhole. Size 23¾ x 9½ in. $39.95
H8010. Monterey Arched Mandolin. Resonant tone quality. Accurately fretted ebonized fingerboard. Adjustable bridge. Mahogany shaded gloss finish. 24-to-1 ratio nickel-plated tuning keys. Size 25 x 10 in. $57.50
H8017. Monterey Arched Mandolin. Solid Spruce Top for fine tone quality. Richly shaded mahogany color, polished body with bound edges. Adjustable rosewood bridge. Bound rosewood fingerboard with inlaid position dots. 24-to-1 ratio nickel-plated tuning keys. Size 25 x 10 in. $82.50
H0831. Carrying Case for models listed above. $12.00
H8025. Harmony Baroque Model Mandolin. Sweeping beauty of line — sweeping brilliance of tone and response. The top of the arched body is of close-grained solid resonant spruce. Sunburst shaded finish, highly polished. Bound fingerboard and adjustable bridge are of rosewood. Engraved headpiece. 24-to-1 ratio nickel-plated tuning keys. Size 28 x 10 in. $119.95
H835. Harmony Baroque Electric Mandolin. Same as Model H8025 except it is made for acoustic or electric playing. The GoldenTone pickup is adjustable and fully guaranteed. Has individual tone and volume controls. Size 28 x 10 in. $149.95
H0835. Carrying Case, Keratol covered, plush lined for Baroque models. $19.50

Harmony's assortment of mandolins ran parallel to their catalog of guitars. In 1968, the line of instruments consisted of three basic models. The No.417 and No.410 Montereys shared the quality of the Monterey line of archtops and were an excellent choice for students. Harmony also sold an "A" style No.331 Stella Lute style mandolin with a flat top and back along with painted binding. It reflected the Stella budget line of guitars.

Circa 1960s Harmony No.417 Monterey was one of the more popular mandolins.

Circa 1960s Harmony H425 Baroque model mandolin.

Circa 1960s Harmony Stella mandolin followed the tradition of the Stella family of instruments.

Harmony was there to inspire students who wanted to explore the joy of playing different instruments. They were able to provide a variety of folk instruments, and are still inspiring a great number of musicians today.

Circa 1960s Harmony H35 electric mandolin. "Carefully designed for excellent mandolin tone and for clean amplification of the tone."

CHAPTER 14

HARMONY REISSUES

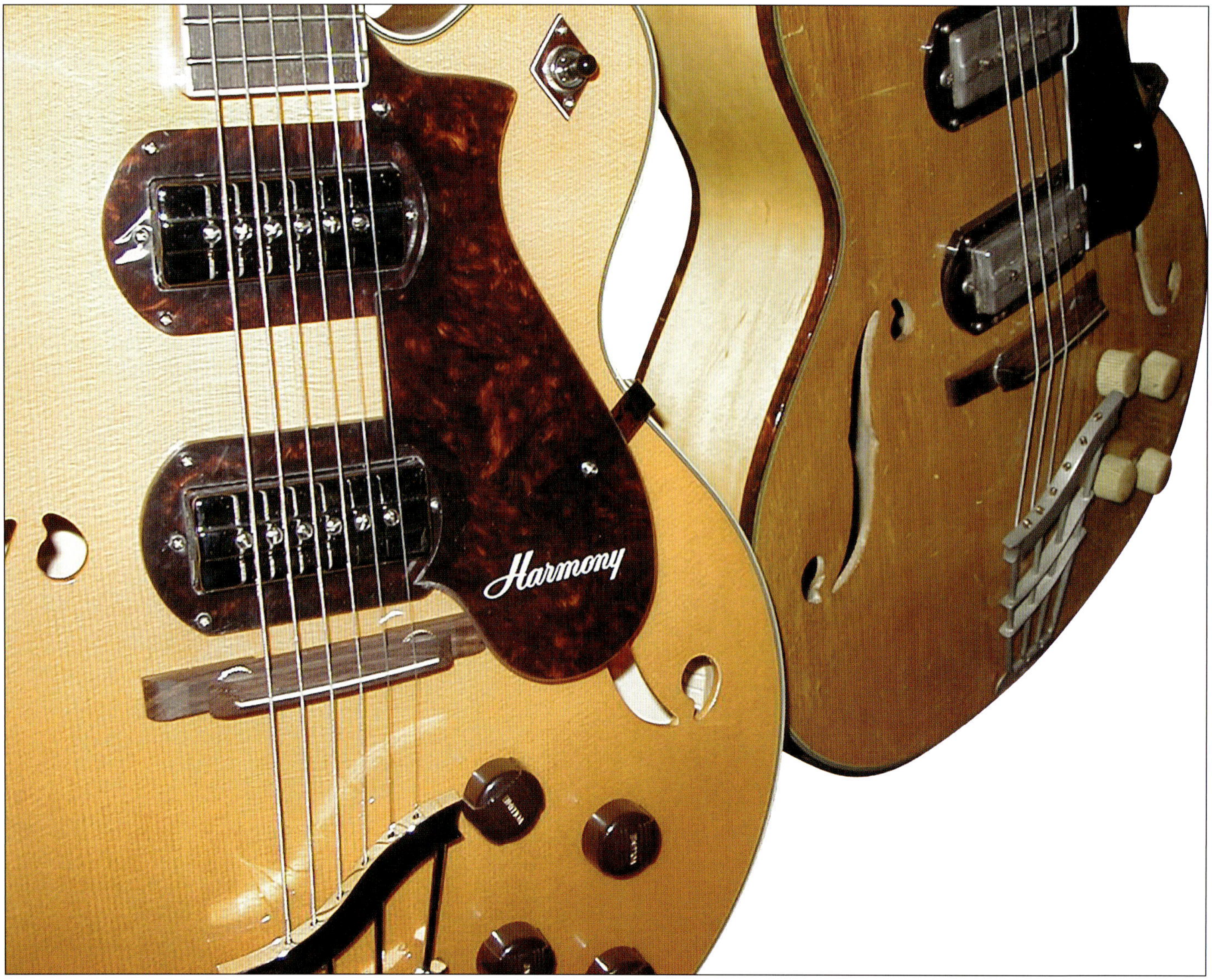

Harmony®
Re-issue
Collection
ST929
Spring '01
HAR59RD
September '01
HARHAWAII
September '01
H22
September '01
– Limited Lifetime Warranty –

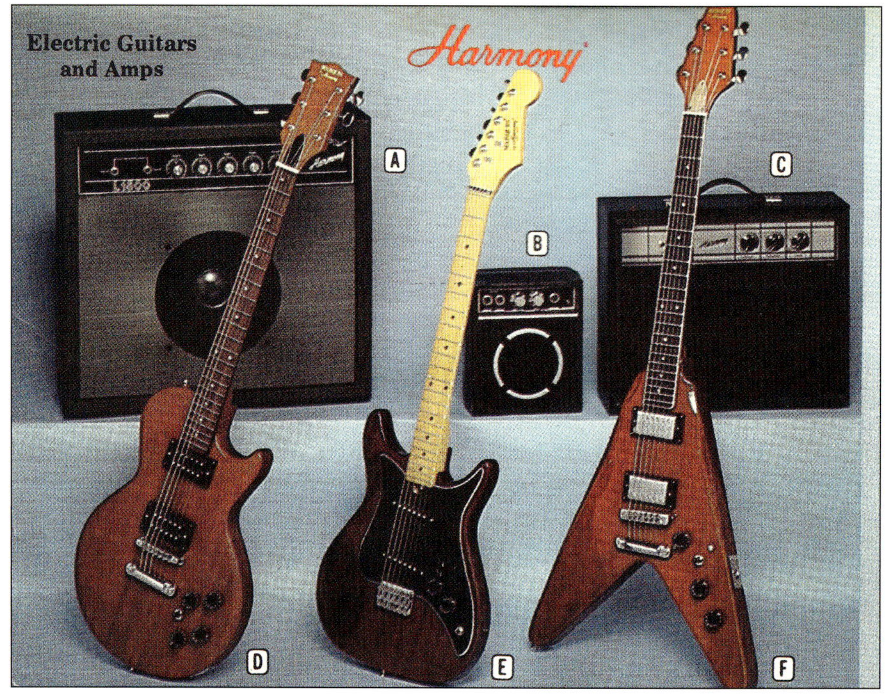
Electric Guitars
and Amps
Harmony
A
B
C
D
E
F

The Harmony name never went away. Throughout the 1980s, there was an assortment of instruments imported with only the Harmony name associated with it. These were copies of traditionally made electrics and inexpensive acoustics, and did not come close to keeping up with the design or quality and appeal of the original product line. These guitars were similar to other Asian made instruments, with no real character, that were distributed through various wholesalers. They seemed to just put the Harmony brand on any instrument.

Marquis was one of the model names used by Harmony on some of the early imports.

Circa 2000 MBT International reissue Stella by Harmony was a limited production, true to the classic Stella design.

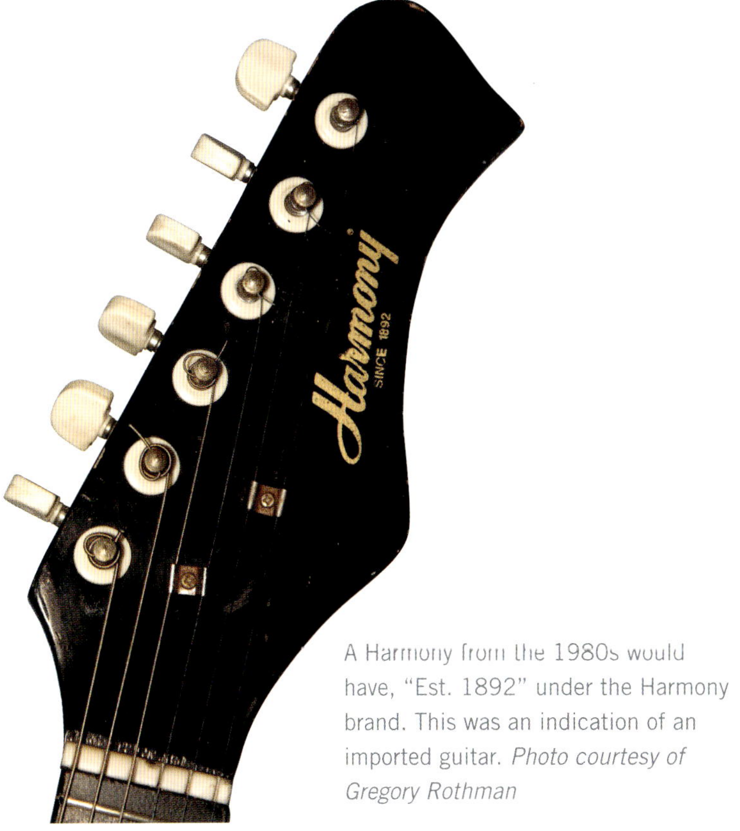

A Harmony from the 1980s would have, "Est. 1892" under the Harmony brand. This was an indication of an imported guitar. *Photo courtesy of Gregory Rothman*

Harmony Guitars and Mandolin

Harmony Rocket
- Electric guitar
- Hollow body
- Maple top, sides, and back
- Hard maple neck
- 3 Humbucking pickups
- 3 Volume and 3 tone controls
- Black finish

Dlr. Net
299[99]

HAR59BK Black
List $699.99
Sell for as low as $499.99 MAP

Limited Edition

Harmony Rocket
Re-introducing the American Legend

Only 100 to be sold

A grand attempt came about to bring back the Harmony guitars we knew, at the turn of the millennium. This was brought about through a bold effort by MBT International to revive the name and product line. Their enthusiastic plan was to reintroduce Harmony models that were produced over the years. MBT's schedule of reissues made Harmony enthusiasts look forward to seeing brand new Rockets, Stratotones, and Sovereigns. Only one hundred or so of the three pickup Harmony Rockets were produced. Other than the original Stella H929 acoustic, the rest of the Harmony instruments were still nothing more than inexpensive imports utilizing the Harmony name.

Circa 2000 Harmony three-pickup Rocket imported by MBT International was black in color and one of the better sounding Rockets I have owned.

Circa 2008 Harmony reissue H50 Spanish electric guitar.

Vintage GUITAR SERIES

H49 STRATOTONE JUPITER

1958-1965

Body	Spruce Top, Maple Sides
	Flamed Maple Back
Neck	Maple
Fing... ...rd	Rosewood
P...	2 Harmony Gold Foil
...ntrols	2V, 2T, 1B, 3 way Switch
Bridge	Floating Adjustable Wooden Bridge
Frets & Scale	20F, 24 1/8"
Machine Heads	Kluson Tuners
Hardware	Chrome
Color	Natural (H49CN)

The 2008 reissue Harmony guitars, with their updated features and hardware, did a great job of recreating the essence and feel of the earlier vintage Harmony instruments. They had the look; they did a good job of capturing the sound, and were made to meet the needs and expectations of contemporary players. How the guitar playing public embraces these guitars will dictate how well they will be received by the new and old generations of Harmony guitar fans in years to come.

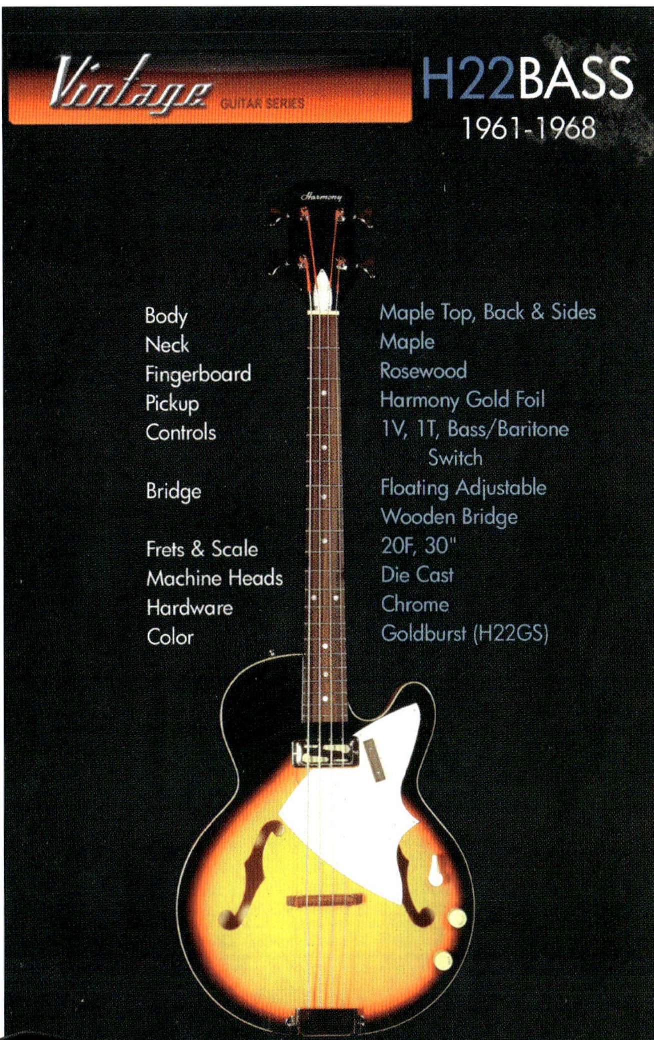

Vintage GUITAR SERIES

H22BASS
1961-1968

Body	Maple Top, Back & Sides
Neck	Maple
Fingerboard	Rosewood
Pickup	Harmony Gold Foil
Controls	1V, 1T, Bass/Baritone Switch
Bridge	Floating Adjustable Wooden Bridge
Frets & Scale	20F, 30"
Machine Heads	Die Cast
Hardware	Chrome
Color	Goldburst (H22GS)

Circa 2008 Harmony reissue H22 bass had larger tuner machines and a set neck making it a more playable guitar.

These new guitars were a nicely crafted instrument that lived up to my expectations in sound and quality. The primary difference of the new guitars is that they were made with a set neck. This differs from the original, vintage USA Harmony, but made for a superior instrument. The new H22 bass also featured better bass tuner machines, which made for easier tuning and gave it the feel of a better quality guitar.

Vintage GUITAR SERIES

H62ARTIST
1954-1964

Body	Spruce Top Flamed Maple Back & Sides
Neck	Maple
Fingerboard	Rosewood
Pickup	Harmony Tone Emphasizers
Controls	2V, 2T, 3 way Toggle
Bridge	Floating Adjustable Wooden Bridge
Frets & Scale	20F, 25 1/8"
Machine Heads	Kluson Tuners
Hardware	Chrome
Color	Goldburst (H62VS) Blonde (H62CN)

Circa 2008 Harmony reissue H62 Artist guitar tried to be a faithful reproduction of the original H62.

Recent imported Harmony "Buck Owens" style Sovereign, made in China.

The short-lived series of Korean made imports were all that were produced during this phase of the Harmony brand. Shortly after these guitars were produced, the company was sold to Westheimer Corporation. The market demand, and time, will tell where they will be in the future, and what might be available.

Circa 2008 Harmony reissue H59 Rocket with three pickups.

CHAPTER 15

MUSICIANS AND THEIR HARMONY GUITARS

Harmony Guitars "Like your first teenage crush ...you never forget"...... Jimmy Vivino. *Photo Credit: Barre "Skills" Duryea*

There are a great number of guitar players who started with or played a Harmony guitar, along with contemporary musicians who were not yet born while Harmony USA was producing guitars. Whether it was a Stella acoustic, Harmony Bob Kat or Rocket Electric, these guitars inspired (or frustrated) many a musician. Session players such as Louis Shelton got his first guitar for his ninth birthday, a $13.00 Stella.

> "I'll never forget my first guitar which was a Stella. I believe it was 1949, as a poor nine-year-old in the backwoods of Arkansas. It was a birthday gift from my older sister and the greatest gift I've ever received. I learned to play on that guitar and two years later upgraded to a Harmony Monterey."

His inspiration to make music might have come from this experience. As he went on to play or produce music with the Monkees and Seals and Crofts, his introduction to guitar playing was on a Harmony.

Harmony had a hard time getting away from the stigma of being a cheaper beginner's guitar, even though there were still plenty of professional musicians who started with and later went on to use them on recordings and in concerts. The musicians who played them must have found the sound desirable and thought enough of these guitars to use them on recordings and in live performances.

Going back to the early days when endorsees like Roy Smeck and Johnny Marvin associated themselves with Harmony guitars, there were a number of other players who also used them. As time went on, country artist Buck Owens had his own Harmony "Artist" model. Contemporary artist Ryan Adams, today, is using one of these Buck Owen guitars for performing. Ryan Adams can choose any instrument to help define himself musically, but he chooses to use a Harmony Buck Owens or Black Sovereign H1264.

Photo courtesy of the Buck Owens Private Foundation and Lee Ann Enns

Circa 1960s Harmony Buck Owens "American," modeled after Buck Owens' Gibson made guitar.

Early blues player Mississippi Fred McDowell was playing a Harmony H1215 Archtone when he was first discovered and recorded in 1959. Big Joe Williams was also seen using a Harmony Sovereign.

During the 1950s, Richie Valens used an H44 Stratotone, a guitar that his name would later become associated with. One of the 2008 reissues was dedicated to him.

In the early days of rock and roll, artists like the Rolling Stones, Spencer Davis, and the Kinks, among others, were using Harmony guitars to define themselves. Dave Davies used a Harmony Meteor for the Kinks recording of "You Really Got Me," in 1962. He had many choices of instruments to use that worked for the music he was creating, yet he chose a Harmony guitar. The tone of this guitar set him apart and helped to characterize his music.

"My first guitar was a blonde Harmony Meteor that my mother bought on the knock (meaning she bought it on a payment plan) . I used it up right up to and after the 'You Really Got Me' and 'All Day and All of the Night' sessions. I used it to play my famous guitar sound and solos on 'You Really Got Me,' 'All Day and All of the Night,' and 'So Tired of Waiting for You.' I must have put it in part exchange for a Gibson or Epiphone, I can't remember. I was in love with it because it was my first ever electric guitar. It was great, I was a kid, I didn't know, it worked! It had a semi-acoustic body and it used to feed back a lot which I liked. I never saw anyone else with one."

Photo courtesy of Dave Davies

Brian Jones of the Rolling Stones played a Harmony Stratotone, which was quite popular in the UK at this time. Keith Richards also was known to play a Harmony Meteor.

Pete Townsend of The Who was another musician who used a Harmony. He had use of a H1270 12-string guitar for writing, recording, and performing. A behind-the-scenes sound that we all have heard on recordings by The Who, and probably did not even realize was a Harmony guitar. It was used on cuts including "Sunrise" and "Sparks/Underture" from the Who's classic rock opera, "Tommy." Townsend was quoted in an *Acoustic Guitar* magazine article as to why he liked this guitar:

> "My first good guitar was an acoustic made in Prague. Later I bought a Harmony 12-string that became my staple. I was a huge fan of Lead Belly, and the Harmony was as close as I could get to his big Stella."

Nashville studio musician Michael Rhodes with his Harmony reissue bass.

Andrew Bazely playing his Harmony H77

Bruce G. Keidler playing his Harmony guitar.

David Berson playing a Harmony Stratone.

Ross Fairweather introducing the next generation to his Harmony archtop.

Russel Trent jamming on a Stratone.

Joe Stone playing his 12-string Harmony guitar.

Cliff Gater playing his Harmony guitar.

JJ Cale cover utilized the image of a Harmony H162 acoustic guitar.

J.J. Cale was another musician that used a modified Harmony guitar for many of his recordings and on stage. The Harmony headstock graphic appeared, in part, on the cover of his "Troubadour" LP.

> "My favorite guitar is this old fifty dollar Harmony, now backless for easier access to the electronics. Originally it was a round hole acoustic, but I've added five pickups for making records and playing concerts. Four of the pickups are Gibson, two of which are low impedance for recording direct. The other bar type pickup came from a Sears Silvertone guitar. It was manufactured by Danelectro. The guitar has three high impedance outs and one low."

Over the years there have been a number of artists who have been seen playing a Harmony guitar. They used them on stage, for performances, and in movies. Jimmy Page used a Harmony Sovereign for an acoustic set on a Led Zeppelin tour in 1971 of Hawaii and Japan. A Harmony H1260 was used for one of the guitar parts for the recording of "Stairway to Heaven." This is an iconic rock and roll song riff, recorded with a Harmony Guitar.

> "The Harmony guitar is quite special to me. It is what I used to write all the acoustic songs and many of the electric songs on the first three albums. I also used it to record all the acoustic tracks on the third album, and it's the guitar I played on 'Stairway to Heaven.' I pretty much used it until I started playing a Martin on *Houses of the Holy.*"

> "What did I like about it? It helped me come up with all these amazing songs! [laughs] It encouraged me. It didn't fight back, and it didn't go out of tune. It would say to me, 'Go on, man, give me more! C'mon!' (Brad Tolinski interview, http://www.guitarworld.com)

Elvis Presley used an H165 acoustic in the 1962 movie *Girls, Girls, Girls* and could be seen playing a H950 Harmony Monterey Archtop in the 1960 film *GI Blues.* He played a Harmony Tenor guitar in a scene from the 1966 United Artists film *Frankie and Johnny.* These were all opportunities to use any instrument available, and he chose to use a Harmony guitar. Even more recently in the 2007 movie *Juno,* Ellen Page (Juno) makes a reference to her "Harmony" guitar.

Rob Stoner was able to move on from the inconvenience of learning on these "Guitar Shaped Objects" and was not discouraged from going on to make music.
Photo courtesy of Rob Stoner

When Bob Dylan went into seclusion after his motorcycle accident in 1966, the "house guitar" at the Big Pink was a Harmony Stella. It was passed around, used and played by members of The Band. They would use this guitar to work on the songs that ended up on the *Music from the Big Pink* recordings.

Elvis Costelo played a Harmony Sovereign when he was starting out playing in the coffee houses in Liverpool. When he produced the 2015 *Lost Basement Tapes* for Showtime, he chose to use a Harmony H1265 Sovereign for some of the tracks. The unique look and ladder braced guitar sound helped define the music that came from the lost Dylan songs.

He responded to a question and answer session on his website when asked: "Out of all the guitars you've used through the years, which are your most beloved?"

> "Most guitars have few good tunes in them-my old Harmony Sovereign contained much of *My Aim is True*.

Rob Stoner who was one of Bob Dylan's bandleaders played a Harmony archtop in his early days, along with a Stella. Use of these budget guitars to learn on did not discourage him from going on to make music.

"That big 'F' hole guitar was OK for a twelve-year-old beginner, until I realized how the cheap manufacturing made it hard to learn on. I also had a smaller Stella with a round hole. By the time I moved up to a decent solid body electric (Epiphone Olympia), I found how much those Chicago-made GSOs (guitar shaped objects) had been impeding my progress. I relegated those Harmony relics to knock around beach guitars and wall decorations."

John Sebastian playing a Harmony H1260 at Woodstock.

Vince Lee has been using Harmony guitars to help define his music across the UK and Europe. *Photo credit: Brian Sherwen*

During the Woodstock Music Festival in 1969, on Saturday afternoon about 3:30 PM, John Sebastian was asked to go on and perform a short set replacing Tim Hardin, who was not able to go on stage. Sebastian, who did not have his guitar, was handed Tim's Harmony H1260 Sovereign. He proceeded to go out on stage, in front of the almost half of a million people who were there, and perform five songs on this guitar. When I asked about this he claimed, "I'm not much of an authority on Harmonys." He did not have to be an expert to appreciate that what he did would become an iconic part of the music that took place that weekend and it was played on a Harmony guitar.

John Sebastian set list from Woodstock, played on a Harmony Guitar

"How Have You Been"
"Rainbows Over Your Blues"
"I Had a Dream"
"Darlin' Be Home Soon"
"Younger Generation"

Even today, contemporary artists are choosing Harmony guitars to define themselves musically. In recent times, the Black Keys guitarist Dan Auerbach has used a variety of Harmony guitars including an H76, a Meteor, and a Stratotone. Another model that has become associated with a specific contemporary artist was the Silvertone (Harmony-made) 1446 that Chris Isaak used; it has now become known as the "Chris Isaak" model. This unique guitar featured Gibson-made mini-humbuckers and a Bigsby tailpiece; it was (and still is) a very usable guitar.

Jimmy Vivino, Conan O'Brien's bandleader, was quoted in *Vintage Guitar* magazine as saying:

> "I love my Harmony Rocket and my Meteor which is a great sounding guitar. I'd always wanted a Harmony Sovereign because a lot of the old blues guys played those, and I got one from '62 or '63. I had it restored and it plays great."

Contemporary indie artist St. Vincent (Annie Clark) can be seen playing a Harmony Bob Kat. She is an artist who established herself after the fall of the Harmony Guitar Company and uses one today to help define who she is.

The Harmony sound still has an appeal and is still able to find its way across the Atlantic, even today. There is a core group of European performers who are using the Harmony look and sound to define themselves. Vince Lee from the UK uses an Espanada, among other Harmony guitars, for the jump blues that he performs. The appeal of the guitar sets him aside from many of the musicians who perform regularly across Europe.

> "I first heard about Harmony guitars (like a lot of like-minded players in my age group) after hearing jump blues guitarists such as Junior Watson, Kid Ramos, Nick Curran, Teddy Morgan, and Rick Holmstrom back in the 1980s and 1990s. It seemed every cool guitarist on the west coast and throughout Texas was playing either a 1950s H-44 Stratotone or an H-62/Espanada archtop. I had always been an archtop player but as a working musician I found myself unable to afford the vintage Gibsons I craved as a young guitarist. In the early days of the Internet I became slightly obsessed with Harmony guitars but the more sought-after models were hard to come

> by in the UK. Over the years I've turned many players on to Harmony guitars in my local blues scene and beyond. My main guitars for live shows would be the H-44 and my Silvertone branded Espanada. I am constantly asked about my guitars at shows."

There have been a number of musicians who are using the recent reissues. The Harmony website lists Jackson Browne, Rick Rosas (Neil Young), Stu Kimball (Bob Dylan), and John Oates (Hall and Oates) as all using the new Harmony guitars to define who they are. Nashville session musician Michael Rhodes bought a reissue Harmony H22 bass from me so he could explore the special place these guitars have in today's music. I can see why; these new guitars play well and give a unique appearance and sound to a performance. That is why I choose to use a Harmony H22 for some of my shows. Not only are these Harmony reissues great guitars, but also they allow you to differentiate yourself from all the players who use the same old "core" Gibson and Fenders.

What Harmony guitars did offer the public was an affordable guitar that would be able to bring music into the American home. These guitars were played and used for making the music they were designed for. As time went on, they became discarded because their utilitarian purpose had been used up.

The ones that survived have been rediscovered by a generation of guitar players who can appreciate the music that can be made with them and the beauty of these instruments, by a guitar company that "Produced millions of instruments ... one at time," and "thus has created thousands of friends for Harmony all over the world."

CONCLUSION

The Harmony story has continued long after the Chicago factory closed down and it continues today. Long after the final parts, tools, and equipment were auctioned off, the Harmony name has carried on.

The Harmony name never really went away. The company and brand have been used, and instruments with the name have been produced in several different reincarnations.

As 2008 rolled around, the Harmony guitars we remembered from our youth came back in a new form. The original guitars had an impact on the rock and roll generation of musicians and we could begin to see what effect they might have on the next generation of guitar players. Charlie Subecz's efforts to bring back the Harmony Guitar Company gave us a selection of new Harmony reissues that captured the essence and feel of the guitars we remember. These fourteen reissues were recreations of the more popular electric models. They were authentic in most respects, but all had set necks. This major difference between the reissues and the originals was that the new Harmony guitars were made to be a more playable instrument, while still capturing the feel of a vintage Harmony. Over the last few years, as I have played a few of the different Korean-made guitars, I have come to realize how much better the Harmony necks are and how much better they play. I have found this to be the most important factor with any guitar, they must be able to be played and used for their intended purpose, to make music.

Harmony guitars have been etched into the musical landscape of America since their origin in the late 1800s. They became a bigger part of our world through the twentieth century as guitar music became more a part of the American home. In each era of their history they catered to the musical trends that were taking place. When there was a ukulele boom in the 1920s, they made a great number of ukes. When violins were in fashion, they made student violins. But nothing made more

where there's music...there's

HARMONY

of an impression on the musical youth of this country than the guitars they produced during the boom that took place with the coming of the Beatles and the era in music history that followed. Folk music and rock and roll both fueled the desire for the youth of America to play guitar. Harmony guitars were able to "find their way into more homes than all other guitar makes combined," and they influenced a whole generation of guitarists and musicians. They strived to bring music to people who might otherwise not have had the means or inclination to learn to play guitar. They inspired countless numbers of young guitarists with their affordable instruments that were meant to be played. At the same time, they worked at creating instruments that appealed to professional musicians, and they succeeded in making guitars that were unique in design with components that succeeded in conveying the music they were chosen to be used for. The famous professional musicians who used them chose them because they were able to deliver the unique sound that helped define who they were and the music they became known for. Harmony guitars were used in all facets of rock and roll, showed up in movies, and they have come to be appreciated by a whole generation of guitar players. You can see this with the number of contemporary players who still choose to use these vintage guitars to help characterize their music. Whether it is one of the better playing reissues or a "teched" up vintage Rocket, these guitars are still here to play and enjoy.

As of today, Westheimer Corporation has been keeping the Harmony brand alive; these guitars are still around, for the time being, as an affordable, playable guitar. Most of the guitars photographed in this book survived in part because they were used to make music and have become a part of the fabric of America's musical youth. Many of them were my guitars that were restored or brought back to life so they could be played. A number of them have been modified, have replaced parts, show repairs and cracks, but most of all they have been loved to the point where they still can be used to make music.

While the famous people who played these Harmony guitars were the ones that inspired, it is the ones that they inspired who credit should be given to. The people who played in the garages and basements of America are the real "rock

stars." They are the ones who made music with these Harmony guitars and kept the brand alive as long as they have by playing these guitars.

It is all about the music; Harmony guitars were an important part of the music that our generation came to love, and will hopefully be here for future generations. After all, as they claimed, "Where there's music, there's Harmony."

Truly the people's guitar!

We've produced Millions of Instruments . . . But we make them One at a time

So you can be sure that, while every Harmony instrument has the same basic characteristics for which all Harmony products are noted, each individual instrument has had dozens of man-hours devoted just to it alone.

—By skilled craftsmen fully trained in innumerable precision hand operations—and the use of most modern equipment—for that closeness-to-perfection which is our constant goal.

—By experienced finishers, who give thoroughgoing individual care to each instrument as it passes through their hands.

—By inspectors, who know that Harmony's heritage of fine instrument making depends on how carefully they check each detail of adjustment and playability before the name Harmony may be affixed to the instrument.

Harmony's extensive stocks of exotic woods—rosewoods from South America, mahoganies from Africa—plus the guitar-type woods from the forests of our own continent—permit our craftsmen the selection necessary to create musical instruments to our exacting standards.

These stocks, largest in the industry, allow for careful seasoning and make available the right types of materials, in the right grades, which help account for the tone, beauty and dependability of the finished Harmony instrument.